# THE SCIENCE & PRACTICE OF COACHING SERIES

# COACHING FOOTBALL'S SPLIT 4-4 DEFENSE

## Pete Noble
## James A. Peterson

COACHES CHOICE™

ISBN: 1-58518-183-8

Book layout : Jeanne Hamilton
Cover design: Rebecca Gold
Diagrams: Michelle R. Dressen
Front cover photo: Provided by *L. A. Times*


Coaches Choice
P.O. Box 1828
Monterey, CA 93942
www.coacheschoiceweb.com

## DEDICATION

This book is dedicated to the people who gave me the confidence and the courage to never quit: my mom, my wife, my brother, Barney, Frank, my children, my coaches, my mentors, my assistant coaches and most important of all my players. I love you all!

And of course, thank you, Dr. Jim.

**P. N.**

# ACKNOWLEDGMENTS

The efforts of the extraordinary staff at Coaches Choice who helped make this book possible are to be commended. We are also grateful to Bob Lambie for his substantial assistance in helping to edit the book.

# CONTENTS

## Chapter

## Appendices:

# FOREWORD

Coach Pete Noble has written THE definitive book on The Split 4-4 Defense. As a result of having employed the defense for 16 years and, winning more than 115 games, Coach Noble reveals all the information that is necessary to effectively implement the principles, concepts, strategies, and tactics of this effective and diversified multiple defense.

Regardless of whether your specific interests lie at the college, junior college, or high school level, anyone with an abiding passion for football will benefit from the information presented within. Pete includes not only the alignments and assignments necessary to teach and play the defense but he also covers the keys and reactions for each front and coverage included in the Split 4-4 package. He will take you through formation and motion adjustments for the defensive line, linebackers, and defensive backs. Just as importantly, you will be privy to the concepts necessary to select and utilize personnel and to combat the diversity of formations, movements, plays and offensive concepts in football today.

Anyone involved in football at any level will learn something from this book.

Ron Lynn
Defensive Coordinator
Washington Redskins

# PREFACE

In 16 years as a head football coach, I have become increasingly aware that the margin between winning and losing is often relatively slim. Without question, one of the most critical factors in a team's success is its ability to implement a sound defensive plan. A sound defense is the by-product of the efforts of a well-prepared, well-organized staff of coaches who are working with players who combine a task-oriented commitment to the job at hand with an indomitable will-to-win.

*Coaching Football's Split 4-4 Defense* was written to provide coaches with the foundation to build a solid defensive plan. The book features special sections on how coaches can organize their coaching staff and can deploy their personnel to develop an organizational plan that will produce a winning program.

*Coaching Football's Split 4-4 Defense* also includes chapters on the skills, techniques, and fundamentals involved in each of the separate position players in the split 4-4 defense—defensive tackle play, defensive end play, inside linebacker play, outside linebacker play and secondary play. In addition, the book presents ten drills which are designed to improve the skills and techniques involved in the split 4-4 defense.

I wrote this book to provide coaches at all competitive levels with a tool that can enable them to maximize the use of the skills and attributes of their players. As such, every coach can benefit from the methods and advice presented in *Coaching Football's Split 4-4 Defense.*

Furthermore, the information presented in this book should be viewed as an erector set—from which coaches can devise additional defensive schemes and plans as appropriate. Coaches should use this information to prepare and execute a success-oriented defensive system. By utilizing the basic principles and ideas presented in this book, every coach will be better prepared to get the most out of his players and to develop a winning program.

**Pete Noble**

# CHAPTER 1

# Understanding the Philosophical Basis of the Split 4-4 Defense

## Criteria for a Successful Defense

Any discussion of the split 4-4 defense must be prefaced with the acknowledgment that there is no singular "best defense" in the game of football. If one exists, every team would be utilizing it. Similar examples can be found in other sports. If there were a single best set of golf clubs, every player on the PGA Tour would have them in his bag. If there were a single best surfboard, every surfer would be riding it. So it is with football defenses. Any number of defensive systems are used successfully at every level of football. Several common features appear to be reflected in all successful defensive systems. At a minimum, it seems that all successful defenses meet the following criteria:

- The defense is fundamentally sound.
- The defense fits a team's personnel.
- The coaching staff has a thorough knowledge of the system.
- The defense is simple to teach, yet difficult to block.
- The coaching staff and the players have an unshakable belief and confidence in the defense.
- The coaches are enthusiastic when coaching the defense.
- The players play hard.

All of these elements are integral components of successful defenses, regardless of whether the alignment is the 5-2, 3-4, 6-1, 4-3, nickel, or split 4-4.

## Historical Perspective

As listed, one of the most important criteria for a successful defense is that it must fit your personnel. Many coaches make the mistake of trying to utilize defenses that have been popularized by college or professional teams without recognizing the fundamental differences between the high school level and the college or professional level. Of paramount importance is the fact that a coach must play with the cards that he is dealt. At the high school level, no drafting of players is held. There isn't (or shouldn't be) any recruiting going on.

That was certainly the case when I was first introduced to the split 4-4 by Bob Erbland in 1976 at Encinal High School in Alameda, California. We had about 1,000 students at Encinal. Because it was next to a naval air station, the student population was extremely transient. We had good athletes but not many large players. One of the advantages of a variable, adjustable defense like the split 4-4 is the ease with which changes can be made to fit the needs of players as well as the coaching staff. Large, strong linemen are a pleasure when you have them, but reality at the high school level is that normally you'll have to make do with smaller, quicker players.

To illustrate the phenomenal success we had with the split 4-4 at Encinal High School, some history is necessary. In 1976 the Encinal High School football program faced many challenges. One of those challenges involved operating under a new head coach. I was on staff in 1975 as the offensive and defensive line coach, and was generally considered the players' favorite to become head coach. However, Bob Erbland came in as head coach and brought the split 4-4 defense with him.

Frankly, our change to the split 4-4 did not occur without some resistance from the returning staff members. Bob came into the office one day and put his defense up on the board. "There is no way we're going to run that," I said. "Why should we change the defense we're running now? This defense is horrible!" We argued with Erbland for three days. "Gentleman, we're going to run this defense, and Noble, you're going to coordinate it, so you better learn to live with it and better learn to like it," he said.

As it turned out, the split 4-4 has been a very, very good defense for me in my career. It got me to Monterey High School where I currently coach. Not surprisingly, the Monterey peninsula is an exceptional place to live and work.

As Erbland's defensive coordinator, I went to work trying to learn all I could about the split 4-4. Fortunately, two local junior colleges were successfully running the defense, so we had a ready resource if needed.

Our 1976 Encinal team was a splintered group. We had player personnel problems, as well as the typical challenges imposed by playing for a new head coach. Nonetheless, our split 4-4 defense immediately made us a more competitive team. Because the defense was new to us, we made coaching errors at each position. However, two advantages of the defense became readily apparent to the staff.

First, it was difficult for our opponents to form a sound blocking scheme against us. Second, our defensive system was very well suited to make changes to fit player personnel as well as coaching staff needs. Although we had a junior-laden team, we finished with a winning record (5-4) and had tremendous success at lower levels.

1977 was a watershed year at Encinal. We went 9-1, winning the first conference championship in school history. That was quite an accomplishment, given that the school opened in 1954. We allowed only seven points per game. Our split 4-4 defense had really arrived.

We had another junior-dominated team in 1978. Although we went 4-5, we played all the teams on our schedule relatively tough on defense. My three-year tenure as defensive coordinator at Encinal ended after the 1978 season. Overall, we were quite pleased that we had gone 18-10 during that period and had established a quality standard of play, especially on defense. As destiny would have it, I was to become head coach at Encinal the next season.

Encinal High School's varsity football team in 1979 was picked in the preseason to finish last in its conference. As Encinal's first-year head coach, I faced a situation where we had only 22 players on the team, and they were mostly junior two-way players. Even though we were picked to finish last in our conference, we had some positives going for us. The coaching staff had returned virtually intact from the previous year. Both freshman-level coaches returned as well as three of four varsity and junior varsity coaches. Only one varsity coach had to be replaced. At that time at Encinal, the varsity and junior varsity practiced together, so we had four position coaches coaching both levels and serving as game day coordinators. Our split 4-4 defense allowed us to score a phenomenal eight defensive touchdowns and helped to propel us to an 8-2 record and a conference championship.

In 1980, Encinal repeated as Alameda County Athletic League champions. We finished 9-3 and were CIF 2A North Coast champions. Two of our losses came after we'd suffered an inordinate number of injuries. We felt like we had the program on track, but we still had only 28 squad members with several individuals playing both ways. 1980 was an especially gratifying year personally. I was also the Encinal wrestling coach, and we won the CIF North Coast Section wrestling championship. No coach had ever won two different CIF championships in the same year.

Injuries, however, took their toll in 1981 and 1982. As a result, we were only a .500 football team over those two years. Not surprisingly, it was especially gratifying when we once again captured the conference championship in 1983. We finished 10-1 despite one of our players suffering a serious spinal injury prior to the playoffs—an occurrence that had a very adverse impact on team morale. Our split 4-4 defense held our opponents to six points per game, and I felt like we played the best man-to-man defense in our league.

In 1984, we were even better defensively. We held our opponents to five points per game and broke Encinal's 1979 record of eight defensive touchdowns with nine defensive scores. We finished 8-3 and once again won our conference. In what was to be my last game at Encinal, our defense intercepted a pass and returned it for the go-ahead touchdown with two minutes remaining in the game. The play got called back for roughing the passer, however, and we eventually lost the playoff game 22-18. Although it was a difficult way to finish our run at Encinal, overall we were proud to have gone 43-18-2 over the six years. More importantly, we had established our split 4-4 defense which was to be the basis of the success we would have at Monterey High School in the coming years.

In 1985, I accepted the head football coaching position at Monterey High School in Monterey, California. The school had an enrollment of 1150, similar in size to Encinal. Most imposingly, however, was the fact that we faced the challenge of taking over a program that had not had a winning season in ten years.

Because Monterey had a five-man varsity and junior varsity football staff, for the first time in my head coaching career, I could properly divide the linebacker coaching responsibilities into separate inside and outside duties. At Encinal, we had only four coaches. Only one coach each worked with the defensive line, defensive backs, defensive ends, and linebackers respectively. The coach working with the linebackers had the most challenging assignment because he had to handle both the inside and the outside linebackers. This predicament was not an ideal situation, but thankfully we had a coach who was a strong, sound fundamentalist who was demanding on his players. Another personnel benefit at Monterey was the fact that we had three-man freshman coaches staff who helped scout our opponents.

We stumbled to a 3-7 record our first year at Monterey. Physically, it was the weakest team I had ever coached. Furthermore, there were many things the players had not been taught. As a result, we had to spend an inordinate amount of time on fundamentals and had to eliminate parts of our defensive package. Nonetheless, we were competitive in every game because of the split 4-4. The split 4-4 defense forced turnovers and confused our opponents. Although we struggled at the varsity level, the stage was set for future success when our junior varsity team went 7-3 and our freshmen were undefeated, finishing 10-0. The following season, we shut out our first four opponents, but our junior-dominated team could do no better than 4-6. Our offense turned the ball over an incredible 56 times in six games. Turnovers are absolutely lethal in high school football because of the relatively short, 12-minute quarters. Our only competitive edge that year was our defense. We finally broke though in 1987, winning a conference co-championship and becoming a CIF Division 3 finalist. Our split 4-4 allowed us to score five defensive touchdowns and to hold our opponents to six points per game. Our only loss in 1987 came in our final game when two bad center snaps cost us nine points in a 12-10 loss. One of the bad snaps literally went out of the stadium. We finished 11-1-1 and had accomplished what some had said couldn't be done. We won a conference championship!

When I arrived at Monterey High School in 1985, many people in the community felt we would never win a conference title, so it was especially gratifying when we repeated as conference co-champions in 1988. Again, our defense was outstanding, yielding only six points per game and producing four defensive scores. We won the conference outright in 1991 with a 9-3 record. In addition, we were a semi-finalist in CIF Division 3. Outstanding years followed in 1993 and 1994 as our teams were 12-1 and 10-2 respectively. The 1993 team was CIF Division 3 champion. The 1994 team was again a CIF Division 3 semi-finalist and recorded 38 sacks for the season.

We finished our first ten years at Monterey 76-34-2. I mention our record not to exclaim how good we were, but to illustrate what I believe the split 4-4 defense accomplished for us. Our teams had become widely renowned for employing a sound, aggressive, attacking defense.

Our defensive philosophy at Monterey had been to stick with our base defense. Although we schemed every opponent and had a defensive package put in each week, we wanted to stay in our base defense as long as we could. Not having to make defensive adjustments during a game meant that our team was in control and our players were able to build confidence in their ability to control the game. We had coached coaches, and coached them hard. The result of our efforts were demonstrated on the field.

## Why the Split 4-4?

Because coaches at most competitive levels are forced to play with the players who are available, it is advantageous to incorporate a defensive system that stresses and utilizes quickness, speed, and strength, rather than size. While quickness, speed, and strength can be developed and improved to some degree, size cannot.

One problem that most high school football programs face is a lack of sizable defensive linemen. In the split 4-4, however only two down defensive lineman are needed. These defenders need to be large enough or quick enough to not get turned, base blocked, or trapped. As a rule, a team almost always has more quick players than large ones. When quickness, speed, and strength are utilized more than size in the defensive line, developing depth at that position is much easier. Greater depth can offer a coach several benefits. At a minimum, it should lead to increased level of consistency of play, since shuffling of players and moving players from other positions should occur less frequently.

The high school coaches' reality is that he often must "make do" with players who are around 5'8" and 165 pounds. Fortunately, this type of player can be very effective in the split 4-4 if he is quick and agile. Because the split 4-4 is an attacking defense by nature, quickness, speed, strength, and agility are paramount components over size. If a team has sizable players who possess the aforementioned attributes, it is strictly a bonus.

Our split 4-4 is not a gap-oriented defense. We key backs. Although we will try to control gaps, we have an aiming point. We attempt to take something away from the offense with our quickness. What we try to take away changes from week to week, and game to game.

The alignment of the front eight defenders in a split 4-4 defense creates very difficult blocking angles for an opponent's offense. Specific alignments will be discussed in later chapters. One key point that I'd like to make at this time is that because defensive tackles in a split 4-4 are on the line of scrimmage in #3 techniques, offenses are often forced to double team them. As a result, offenses are usually forced to make changes in their blocking schemes, especially in their trapping game since 4-4 plays trap backside hard.

One of the basic tenets of our defensive philosophy is that we want to stop the run first. The eight-man front of the split 4-4 affords maximum run support. There is always an extra attacking defender at the offensive point of attack.

The alignment and angles of the split 4-4 are very conductive to blitzing and overloading blocking schemes. Specific blitz packages are covered in Chapter 9, but the tactical possibilities are almost endless. We can cover all the inside and outside gaps with our front eight. Blitzes often can confuse offenses, leading in turn to offensive mistakes, turnovers, and general dysfunction by the offense.

Although gaining in popularity, the split 4-4 defense is still an unusual front for most opponents. It is not a defense a team sees every week. Presenting a unique and unorthodox front to an opponent has clear advantages. When confronted by a split 4-4 defense, an offense must teach new blocking schemes to deal with the extra defender. New blocking schemes means spending extra time on offense. Not only must an offense prepare for the base 4-4 split defense, it must also prepare and work on solutions for the defender's blitz package. For an offense, this situation can be very time consuming. As stated previously, we like to stay in our base defense as long as possible. Because the split 4-4 tends to make the offense spend time preparing for possible blitzes, a team may be forced to work on things it won't even use. Furthermore, forcing an opponent's offense into extra preparation time may have a domino effect on a team's entire game preparation. A team may now have less time to devote to other critical areas of the game. At a minimum the whole situation of facing a formidable, but new-type of defensive scheme may breed doubt and anxiety in the minds of opposing players and coaches.

Another advantage of the split 4-4 defense is the fact that the uniqueness of the front usually forces the opponent's offense into simplifying their blocking schemes to deal with the split 4-4 package. Fewer and simpler offensive blocking schemes can provide an advantage for the defense. Defenders know better what to expect and how to react to it.

Another benefit of employing the split 4-4 involves the fact that the base front in the split 4-4 can be split to give additional looks without any change in technique or the accompanying additional instructional time (multiple front option). A coach should keep in mind that the fourth criteria for a successful defense (listed in an earlier section in this chapter) is that the defense must be both simple to teach and must be complex for the offense to block. One of the most common errors of offensive and defensive coaches is adding too much to their respective packages. Too much information tends to confuse players, takes away their aggressiveness (especially on defense), and can be detrimental to execution. Changes in a defensive front may be in response to formation, backfield formation, or rushing tendencies relative to the field position. Changes in the front may also be made to confront specific plays (e.g., the power running game, the option game, the passing game, etc.).

Yet another positive feature of the split 4-4 defense is that it is a variable defense that adapts and adjusts easily to challenges presented by a proficient passing offense. Coverage changes and implementation of nickel and dime coverages are done quite simply. This factor reflects the essential beauty of the defense. Although the split 4-4 presents an eight-man front designed to attack the run, it is easily adjustable to defend the pass.

The split 4-4 is generally a "bend but don't break" defense. We're in a three-deep zone most of the time, but we do have some man coverage. No one will see a clipboard flying on our sideline when our team gives up a 20-yard run. We may give up a 50-yard run. In fact, we once gave up a 90-yard run in a playoff game. We understand that might happen when we're in an eight-man front. The trade off is if a team doesn't have big players, the speed and athletic ability of the available players can be better utilized. The three-man secondary must be ingrained from day one with the fear of getting beat deep.

Lastly, but importantly, is the difficulty offenses can have blocking the split 4-4 on the lower levels. As hard as the defense is to block on the varsity level, it appears that the split 4-4 defense is even more difficult to deal with on the freshman and junior varsity levels. Success on the lower levels can be a critical factor in establishing a consistent winning program. It can also play an integral role in helping to rejuvenate a program that has been down. To reinforce this point, in my 16 years at Encinal and Monterey High Schools, we had only one losing season at the junior varsity level and just two losing seasons on the freshman level.

# CHAPTER 2

# Deploying Your Personnel

## Basic Traits of Effective Defenders

Proper evaluation and deployment of personnel specific to position requirements is a crucial factor in developing a successful defense. Although each separate defensive position requires distinctly different skilled and athletic types, some common criteria relevant to all defenders can be identified. These criteria can generally be categorized into physical skills and mental (or attitudinal) abilities.

### _Physical Criteria_

A defender...

- Should be able to run well.
- Should be able to change directions quickly.
- Should be able to move his feet to avoid obstacles with quickness and agility.
- Should have the strength level commensurate with the position, and/or the ability to effectively use leverage.

### _Mental or Attitudinal Criteria_

A defender...

- Should have the mind-set of playing with maximum intensity and effort on every play.
- Should possess an intelligence level capable of comprehending assignments and responsibilities of the position.
- Should have an inclusive "team" view of his role within the framework of the defense. Use terms "we" or "us," not "I" or "me."

It is important to note that size is not listed as a fundamental physical requirement. As was previously discussed, while a high school coach has almost no control over the size of his players, he can develop the other attributes necessary for the players to be effective defenders. The evaluation and subsequent development of these skills is a key factor in producing an effective defense.

## Position Qualifications for the Split 4-4 Defense

Identifying the proper player for a particular position is one of the most important responsibilities a coach can perform. The split 4-4 defense employs four defensive linemen—two defensive tackles (T) and two defensive ends (E); four linebackers—two inside linebackers (Mike — "M" and Willie — "W") and two outside linebackers (Sam — "S" and Rover — "R"); two cornerbacks; and one safety. The alignment of these players in the base split 4-4 defense is illustrated in Diagram 2.1. The better a coach understands the basic qualifications for each position player category in the split 4-4 defense, the more likely the coach will place the right players in the right position.

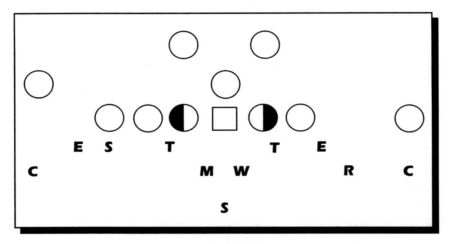

**Diagram 2.1**
**Split 4-4 Defense (40 Base)**

## Defensive Tackles

The best big men should be placed at the defensive tackle position. These players must be either physically strong or quick enough to absolutely not get turned or base blocked. Although height is not overly important, it is important to keep in mind that a short player may lose the quarterback landmark against tall offensive linemen. Defensive tackles must be agile enough to squeeze the trap play and to move laterally down the line to make plays. Strength, quickness, and the ability to use leverage can compensate for lack of size. We've had some tremendous smaller players at this position who were superior technicians. When a coach has larger players with quickness, it is a definite bonus.

## Defensive Ends

Defensive ends are two-point-stance, stand-up players in the split 4-4 defense. Individuals selected to play defensive end do not have to be the most physical players, but they must be agile and disciplined. The defensive end position is probably the easiest position to play in the split 4-4. We use what we call "real old kind" defensive ends. They're not outside linebackers, they're *defensive ends.* That means they attack the quarterback on an option play, attack upfield, contain the quarterback on the pass rush, and squeeze the field. Unlike many coaches who feel that defensive ends are basically linebackers, we feel that these players require specific skills and abilities. The mind set and techniques of defensive ends are different than linebackers. Basically, we're looking for players who are quick and agile enough to play linebacker, but who can still take on a kick-out block from the power play and squeeze it down.

## Inside linebackers

The inside linebacker positions in the split 4-4 should be manned by true "inside linebacker types." This term implies that an aggressive, physically strong player is needed to play inside linebacker. An inside linebacker should not be overly aggressive or he will not be able to make the proper backside reads. A "nose for the ball" and good football sense are requisite qualities for linebackers who need to be able to shed blockers and take correct paths to the ball.

In our split 4-4 defense, "Mike" is the strongside inside linebacker, while "Willie" is the weakside inside linebacker. These two defenders will flip sides according to the formation the offense is in. Mike is generally the stronger of the two and usually calls the signals. In that regard, he must be willing to spend more time than any other defensive player studying video tape and scouting reports on his opponent. He must be a communicator. The Mike position on defense is roughly analogous to the quarterback position on offense. The defender who assumes the role of Mike must be the vocal, emotional, and physical leader of the defense and must assume the inherent responsibilities of that role.

## Outside Linebackers

The Sam linebacker in our split 4-4 defense is the strongside outside linebacker. He will flip flop to the tight-end side or the strength of the formation. All factors considered, we want our best defender on the team lined up at this position. Size is not a factor if the player is smart and understands how to use leverage.

The best player we ever had at the Sam position was a 5'9" college-prep type at Encinal named Leonard. Although we've had two Sams who played Division 1 college football, this guy was better. Leonard was an extremely intelligent player whose father was a colonel in the Marine Corps. He went on to college at Cal Poly, but did not continue to play football although he was the best outside linebacker I've seen in this defense. In Leonard's junior year, he had to play against Roderick Jones from El Cerrito High School, who eventually started for the University of Washington. Roderick almost killed him. The next year as a senior, Leonard owned Roderick because he got underneath Jones' pads. Fortunately for Leonard, Leonard knew how to use leverage!

The outside linebacker to the weakside of the formation is called Rover. Rover can be either a fourth linebacker or a fourth defensive back on your team. The Rover position can accommodate a wider range of athletic types, depending on what a coach feels he will be confronted with offensively in his conference. Generally, Rover is a strong safety, monster-back type of player who must be able to provide support versus the run. He also has to be able to defend against the pass, as well as be a rush player because he will blitz in the split 4-4. If he's not a rush player, a defensive team may be giving a little bit away. The bottom line in selecting the Rover is that he must be versatile enough relative to what types of offenses your team will face.

### Cornerbacks

In our split 4-4 system, the cornerbacks are usually among the fastest players on the team and are also proficient tacklers. At a minimum, cornerbacks must be fast enough to meet the physical demands of man-to-man coverage. The corners also need to be aggressive players, but not so aggressive as to cause them to be out of position because of their overzealousness. Exhibiting an appropriate level of aggression is a fine line—one that cornerbacks must constantly approach, but not cross. Furthermore, cornerbacks must be mentally disciplined players. One of their most overriding thoughts must be to never to get beat deep. Good timing and good hands are also requirements of the cornerback position. As a general rule, high school coaches should keep in mind that accomplished basketball players often tend to make good cornerbacks.

### Safety

The safety position is aptly named. Because of the eight-man front in the split 4-4 defense, a team using this defense stands a great risk of a breakaway by the offense. The safety must play "safe." While he does not have to have the foot speed of a cornerback, he must be a disciplined, sure tackler. He may compensate for his lack of foot speed by adjusting his alignment depth, depending on the down and distance and frequency of routes he faces. He must have a "field position and ball sense" about him, much like a centerfielder would in baseball. A patient, unselfish player who can follow directions is required. He must understand the defensive plan. As a general rule, because the safety is in charge of coverage calls and change of coverage decisions, he needs to be an intelligent, extroverted communicator.

## Ideal vs. Reality

The requirements described for the various positions are ideal standards. The high school coach often does not have the luxury of having players who meet all the criteria for every position. The closer a coach can come to placing players in positions where they match the physical and mental criteria for a particular position, however, the more successful the defense is likely to be.

# CHAPTER 3

# Organizing Your Coaching Staff

The split 4-4 is not a defense that should involve assumption. A coach cannot assume that players will magically acquire the knowledge and skill fundamentals necessary to play this defense successfully. These fundamentals must be coached, and coached hard. A coach needs to develop a specific prescription for teaching these fundamentals. It can also not be assumed that all coaches have a satisfactory grasp of the fundamental techniques involved in the split 4-4 defense. As a result, "coaching the coaches" is of primary importance. Coaches need to have a thorough knowledge and confidence in the fundamentals of the defense (refer to criteria #3 in Chapter 1), and must be able to teach these basics effectively.

The split 4-4 defense has many techniques, stances, etc. that are different from traditional defenses. As a staff, an organized plan for inserting all of the defensive techniques involved in the split 4-4 should be followed. We begin with our base split 4-4 defense, which we call 40 Green. We formulate a specific time line for inserting all of our fronts and coverages. The pace of the schedule depends on the rate of learning by the players and the teaching skills of our staff, A coach should not overlook the importance of getting the second- or third-line players involved in drills.

A key point to remember is that a head coach cannot teach the split 4-4 defense all by himself. Position coaches must be able to coach the assigned techniques, hold independent chalk talks by position, etc. with their players.

Most high school situations dictate that coaches coach on both sides of the ball. A list of ideal matchups on a high school varsity/JV staff that has to coach both offense and defense would include the following:

| Offensive Assignment* | Defensive Assignment* |
|---|---|
| • Offensive line ................................................ | Defensive tackles |
| • Quarterbacks ................................................... | Defensive ends |
| • Offensive line ................................................. | Defensive ends |
| • Offensive line ................................................. | Inside linebackers |
| • Receivers ....................................................... | Outside linebackers |
| • Running backs ............................................... | Secondary |

\* All coaches should be involved with special teams.

The quarterback/defensive end coach is also an ideal person to serve as the offensive coordinator. He can run the scout team during seven-on-seven drills, while the defensive-tackles coach can take the defensive ends during that period to work on screen, draw, and pass-rush techniques.

Continuity on the coaching staff is crucial for success. Our junior varsity players went through all of the individual and combo periods with the varsity position coach. Ideally, this individual will be the same coach for a player's entire three-year high school career, so that the same methodology, with upgrades, will be used the entire three-year period.

On our freshman staff, we only have three paid coaches. This situation seems to be fairly typical on the high school freshman level. Defensive responsibilities for a three-man staff may be allotted as follows:

- Defensive line coach
  (responsible for tackles and ends)
- Linebacker coach
  (responsible for Mike and Willie, Sam and Rover)
- Secondary coach

A coach should monitor the freshman level team closely, largely because of the relatively small staff working with this group. With only a few coaches assigned to the freshman team, combination periods must be used creatively to afford maximum opportunities for instruction. The defensive scheme needs to be kept minimally simple. Toward that end, a coach should use the base front and a few simple blitzes.

I have eight paid coaches at Monterey who are all teachers on staff. This extremely fortuitous situation is highly unusual in the cash-strapped California of the 1990s. At Encinal, I only had six coaches. Although it was sometimes difficult, we did very well because of our efforts to communicate and cooperate as much as possible.

## Quality Instruction

At times, a head coach must be a virtual dictator and insist on certain important factors. Quality instruction is one of them. Coaches have to want to improve as much as the players. Show me a coach who knows it all, and I want him on our schedule.

Coaches must be accountable for several aspects of their job, including:

- Offering quality instruction.
- Conducting appropriate drills.
- Providing meaningful repetitions for their players.
- Evaluating their players.

Evaluating players is an important responsibility of the head coach. A head coach should make sure that the evaluation process includes evaluating his coaching staff, as well as his player personnel. Evaluating coaches is somewhat of a subjective matter that should generally focus on the ability of each staff member to help accomplish specific, target objectives that have been established by the head coach. Through almost two decades of coaching, my major goals relative to staff performance are:

- 100% perfect instruction.
- 100% perfect execution.
- 100% unit pride and loyalty.
- Have a ton of FUN!
- Be the hardest workers in the state.
- Provide a quality experience for each player. Coach the way I would want to be coached if I were a player.
- Win the game, but have FUN doing it!

An overview of the specific responsibilities we expect of assistant football coaches and coordinators is presented in Appendix A of this book.

## Making Football Fun

As football coaches in this day and age, we are in competition with all kinds of other sports and activities for the players' time. In order to field competitive teams, we must make the overall experience fun and enjoyable. This factor is often one of the most underrated aspects of successful football programs. Personally, I enjoy surfing. I need to make football at least as enjoyable to me as surfing, otherwise I wouldn't coach. In a similar vein, I want to make the game enjoyable for all of my players.

# CHAPTER 4

# Defensive Tackle Play

As a general rule, a coach should assign his best big defenders to the defensive tackle position. Ideally, a defensive tackle should be tall enough to see his quarterback landmark even over relatively tall offensive lineman. Furthermore, they should be strong or quick enough to avoid being base blocked or turned. In addition, they should be agile enough to squeeze the trap play and to move laterally to make plays.

In general, we require our defensive tackles to adhere to four important rules:

- They cannot get turned.
- They cannot get base blocked one-on-one.
- They cannot get reached/hooked.
- They must squeeze the trap.

### Standard Reference Points for the Defense

The gaps and defensive alignment techniques are lettered and numbered up front so that the coaching staff can instruct and operate standard reference points. The reference point system we employed at Monterey High School is shown in Diagram 4.1. The alignment reference points for the various defensive techniques are presented in Table 4.1.

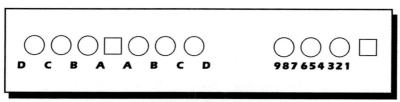

**Diagram 4.1**
**Gap and technique reference points.**

| Technique | Alignment |
|-----------|-----------|
| 1 | inside eye of guard |
| 2 | head up guard |
| 3 | outside eye of guard |
| 4 | inside eye of tackle |
| 5 | head up tackle |
| 6 | outside eye of tackle |
| 7 | inside eye of TE |
| 8 | head up TE |
| 9 | outside eye TE |

**Table 4.1**
**Alignment reference points for specific defensive techniques.**

**Keys and Reactions**

*40 (Base)*

In our base split 4-4 defense (which we call "40"), the defensive tackles are in a three-point stance in a 3 technique. Each defensive tackle has a read technique keying the near back. If the near back comes to him, the tackle plays dive (Diagram 4.2).

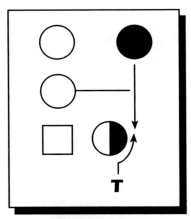

**Diagram 4.2**
**Defensive tackle vs. dive.**

If the near back goes to the end, the defensive tackle checks for a trap/counter play and moves laterally to the C gap (Diagram 4.3).

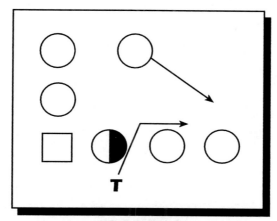

**Diagram 4.3**
**Defensive tackle vs. the near back to**
**the end.**

If the near back goes away, the defensive tackle plays trap, attacking the offensive guard with his near shoulder. The defensive tackle's head is upfield, maintaining outside leverage with his outside arm and leg. He squeezes the trap play with his near shoulder. His landmark is the center's opposite foot. His head and shoulders are square (Diagram 4.4).

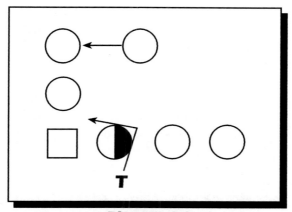

**Diagram 4.4**
**Defensive tackle vs. the near back away.**

It is critical that the defensive tackles must not get base blocked or reach blocked one-on-one by the offensive guard. If the offensive guard is able to base or reach the defensive tackle, it allows the offensive tackle to perform a clean down block on the inside linebacker, thereby cutting off the inside linebacker's pursuit course to the ball. If this situation is allowed to occur, it can present a serious fundamental threat to the defense (Diagram 4.5).

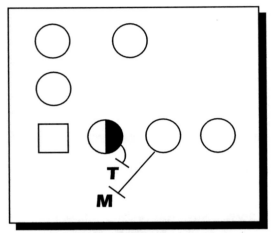

**Diagram 4.5**
**Defensive tackle vs. a base/reach block.**

The initial blow of the tackle should be a hand shiver. We don't teach the rip-up as an initial move. We've found that a defender executing a rip-up move gets lost too quickly, and it's easier for the offensive guard to hold him. In addition, using a rip move makes it more difficult for a defensive tackle to get off the block and provides for too much upfield penetration versus the trap.

Versus a pass, the defensive tackles attack a predetermined landmark on the quarterback. The near tackle attacks the quarterback's outside number or armpit, while the far tackle attacks the quarterback's near number or armpit. They must always stay on track and not get pushed out of their rush lanes (Diagram 4.6). The pass rush is discussed in greater detail in Chapter 9.

Versus a draw play, the defensive tackles must retrace their steps laterally to the line of scrimmage. If the offensive guard is allowing the outside rush path and the defensive tackle senses draw, the defensive tackle must communicate that to his teammates (Diagram 4.7).

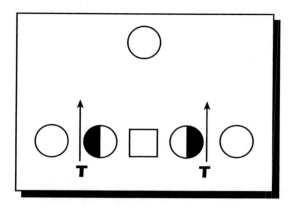

**Diagram 4.6**
**Pass rush by the defensive tacklers.**

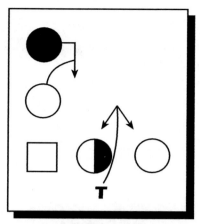

**Diagram 4.7**
**Defensive tackles**
**vs. a draw.**

Versus a screen pass, the away defensive tackle is designated as the rush tackle unless there are two screens. In that case, the away tackle must read and play the screen pass. The near defensive tackle, upon reading the screen, retraces his steps and follows the offensive linemen to their set-up spot. He should hustle to position himself behind the offensive lineman, all-the-while communicating "screen" to his teammates (Diagram 4.8).

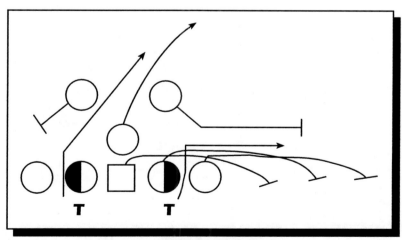

**Diagram 4.8**
**Defensive tackles vs. a screen pass.**

*Change-ups*

The two basic front alignment changes we use are what we call the 60 front and the 50 front. In the 60 front, the defensive tackles align in a 2 technique and execute a "go" technique, which is an aggressive upfield move up the B gap (Diagram 4.9).

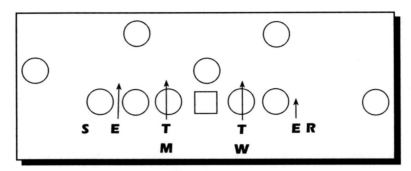

**Diagram 4.9**
**60 defense.**

In the 50 front, the weakside defensive tackle stays in a 3 technique. The strongside defensive tackle (generally aligned on the tight-end side) plays a reading 6 technique (Diagram 4.10).

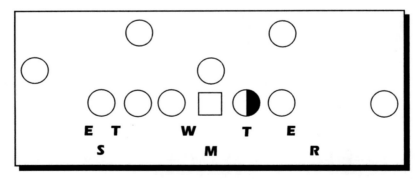

**Diagram 4.10**
**50 defense.**

## Teaching Progression

Philosophically, we prefer to stay in our base 40 defense as long as possible. If we can stay in it and be successful the whole game, we will do so. Therefore, in the teaching progression for defensive linemen, base 40 alignments, techniques, and reactions should be mastered before the introduction of multiple fronts.

# Defensive End Play

The defensive end position is probably the easiest position to play in the split 4-4 defense. While defensive ends do not have to be a team's most physical players, they must be agile. More often than not, defensive ends are more slender than those players who typically play the defensive tackle block position. [In general terms, when we're involved in the process of who should play defensive end, we look for a quick, agile player who can still take on a kick out and squeeze the line of scrimmage to make the field smaller.]

### Keys and Reactions

*40 (Base)*

In the base 40, the defensive ends are stand up, two-point stance players aligned in a 9 technique (Diagram 5.1). On the snap of the ball, a defensive end's inside foot should be up and his outside foot should be back. In the split 4-4 defense, the defensive ends take two read steps and squeeze the line of scrimmage. On his second step, the defensive end should have his outside foot free and his shoulders square with the line of scrimmage.

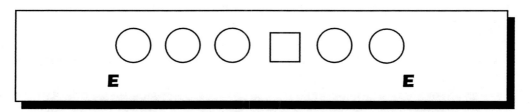

**Diagram 5.1**
**Defensive end alignment.**

Versus an option play, if the quarterback opens towards him, the defensive end attacks the quarterback's numbers, working his head to the quarterback's upfield armpit. The defensive end should engage the quarterback approximately where the offensive guard lined up initially (Diagram 5.2). If the option play is away from the defensive end, the defensive end should trail as deep as the deepest back (Diagram 5.3).

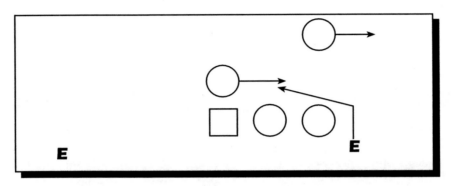

**Diagram 5.2**
**Defensive end play vs. an option play toward him.**

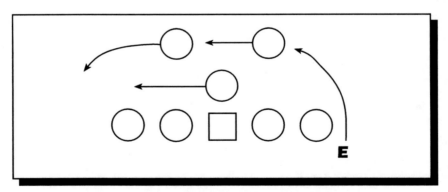

**Diagram 5.3**
**Defensive end play vs. an option play away.**

Versus a power or sprint draw play, the defensive ends should squeeze the field. The defensive ends attack the near back or the fullback with their inside shoulder, while keeping their shoulders square. The defensive ends should maintain outside leverage, while keeping their outside foot and arm free. They must drive the runner back into the hole (Diagram 5.4).

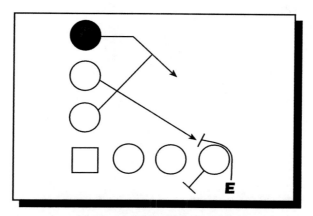

**Diagram 5.4**
**Defensive end play vs. a power/sprint draw play.**

Versus an isolation play, the defensive end again squeezes the play, keying the tailback. He takes on the offensive blocker (tight end, slot, offensive lineman) with his inside shoulder, while maintaining outside leverage for the possibility of a bounce outside by the tailback (Diagram 5.5).

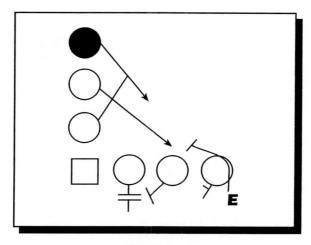

**Diagram 5.5**
**Defensive end play vs. an isolation play.**

Versus a quick toss or sweep play, the onside defensive end must maintain outside leverage by fighting outside. He tries to make the field smaller. He keeps the running back to his inside shoulder, while maintaining his shoulders square. The defensive end must not allow himself to be hooked or crack blocked by a wide receiver. If a team cracks back, the defensive end must take read steps and get straight upfield (Diagram 5.6). If the play goes away, the defensive end again trails as deep as the deepest back (Diagram 5.7).

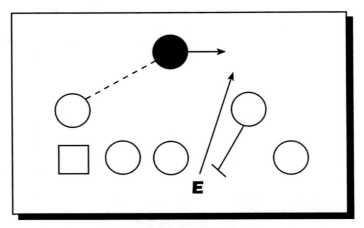

**Diagram 5.6**
**Defensive end play vs. a quick toss or sweep play.**

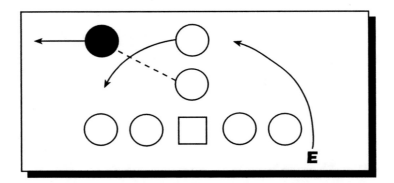

**Diagram 5.7**
**Defensive end play vs. a quick toss or sweep away play.**

Our defensive ends and tackles provide a four-man pass rush. We pair the defensive tackle and end on the same side as a team. The near defensive end's landmark is the quarterback's outside number or armpit. The far defensive end's landmark is the far number or armpit of the quarterback. Similar to the defensive tackles, the defensive ends must maintain their own rush track. They need to take on any offensive back's block with their inside shoulder, while maintaining outside leverage. The defensive ends must contain the quarterback (Diagram 5.8). The pass rush is discussed in greater detail in Chapter 9.

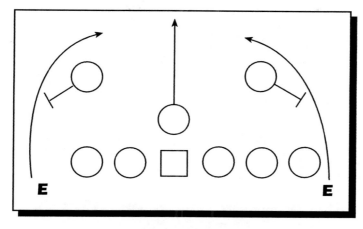

**Diagram 5.8**
**Pass rush by the defensive ends.**

Versus a draw play, the defensive ends retrace their steps and communicate "draw" to their teammates. Against a screen pass, the defensive ends read the near back. If the offensive back releases, the defensive end maintains outside leverage with the back and goes with him. The backside defensive end rushes the quarterback and checks the field (Diagram 5.9).

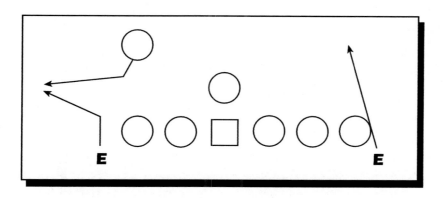

**Diagram 5.9 ends vs. a screen play.**

# Inside Linebacker Play

The most controversial component of our split 4-4 defense is our linebackers. Our inside linebackers are referred to as Mike and Willie. Inside linebackers must be aggressive players and tacklers.

The inside linebackers are positioned at least four yards off the ball, head up on the guard, and take what is called a "read step" on the snap of the football. It is important that the front defensive personnel keep the offensive linemen off of the linebackers. The linebackers must be free to make plays. Mike and Willie align in a two-point stance with their outside foot up. They take their read steps with their inside foot towards the line of scrimmage so that their outside foot becomes free (Diagram 6.1).

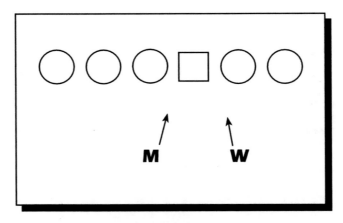

**Diagram 6.1**
**Inside linebacker alignment.**

We may (and have) positioned the inside linebackers back anywhere from four and one-half to six yards deep, depending on their reading and recognition requirements. In general philosophical terms, the inside linebackers need "grass to operate in."

The inside linebackers key their near back. Versus an I formation, they key the fullback. If the near back comes to them, they attack the line of scrimmage (Diagram 6.2).

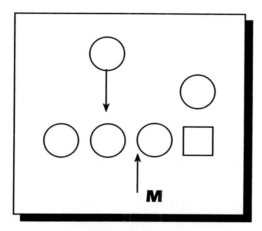

**Diagram 6.2**
**Inside linebacker play vs. a play**
**where the near back comes to him.**

If the near back goes away, the inside linebacker cross keys to the far back and plays the backside trap or counter (Diagram 6.3).

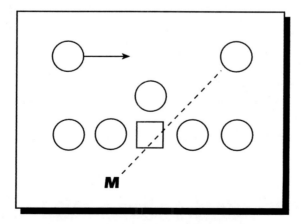

**Diagram 6.3**
**Inside linebacker play vs. a play where the**
**near back runs away from him.**

If all backs go away, the inside linebacker away from the flow keys for the counter or a reverse (Diagram 6.4).

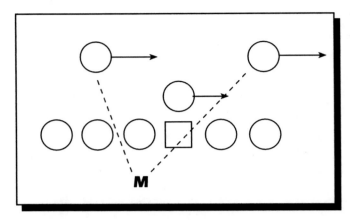

**Diagram 6.4**
**Inside linebacker vs. full flow away.**

Versus a power play, the onside, inside linebacker attacks through the B gap to the C gap. The backside linebacker plays the trap or counter (Diagram 6.5).

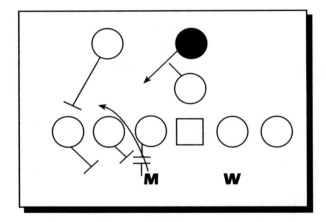

**Diagram 6.5**
**Inside linebacker response to a power play.**

Versus the isolation play, the linebacker attacks the isolation back (generally a fullback) outside in, squeezing the play (Diagram 6.6). Defensively, we should never be trapped, countered, or reversed because we're balanced with two linebackers frontside and two linebackers backside. The linebackers do not cross the center's head until they *know* where the ball is.

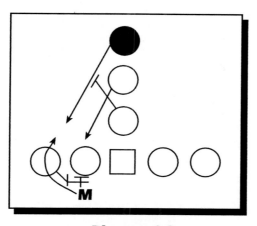

**Diagram 6.6**
**Inside linebacker response to an isolation play.**

Our inside linebackers are coached to stop the run first. Versus pass, they must check for a quarterback sneak and draw first, as well as be cognizant of a screen. When pass is read, the inside linebackers retreat to their hook/curl zones (Diagram 6.7). Typically, the hook area is directly in front of the tight end's position, while the curl zone is just inside the wide receiver's position. The short zones underneath, such as a hook and a curl, have a vertical maximum depth of 15 yards. The method of retreat we teach to our linebackers is to turn their backs to the center of the field and run to their zone-coverage landmarks. The inside linebackers must recognize which backs and receivers can threaten their zones, since the linebackers are dropping with their eyes focused on the quarterback. Because our inside linebackers are responsible for reading the backs, the draw play and the screen play are generally easy reads for the inside linebackers.

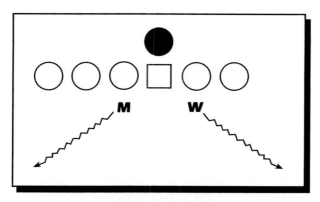

**Diagram 6.7**
**Inside linebacker zone drops vs. a pass play.**

# CHAPTER 7

# Outside Linebacker Play

Our outside linebackers are called Sam and Rover. Sam is the strongside outside linebacker, while Rover is the weakside linebacker.

### Sam Linebacker

The Sam linebacker should be the best defender on the team. During the game, he will flip flop to the tight-end side or to the strength of the formation. Size is not generally a factor at this position. In fact, we have had some outstanding smaller players excel as the Sam outside linebacker.

The Sam linebacker aligns in a two-point stance with his inside foot up, his knees bent, and his weight slightly forward on his toes. Against a tight end, Sam linebacker is in a 8 technique in the line of scrimmage. He attacks the tight end with a read step, using his inside foot. The tight end must not be allowed to release inside (Diagram 7.1). Because of the alignment of the Sam linebacker, we sometimes give the appearance of a five-man front. If the Sam linebacker is having trouble with the tight alignment on the line of scrimmage, the coach should try backing him off one yard. If he still has trouble, the Sam linebacker should work hard on his stance. A good, low stance is critical for the Sam linebacker position, since the tight end must be trapped at the line of scrimmage and must be kept off of the inside linebackers.

**Diagram 7.1**
**Sam linebacker basic alignment.**

Certain situations or formations dictate using a rush-frequency table to determine the strength of formation, and hence, the alignment of the Sam linebacker. These formations include slot, wide, twins, double wing, two tight ends or two split ends.

The Sam linebacker generally cross keys the far back for his key (Diagrams 7.2 to 7.7).

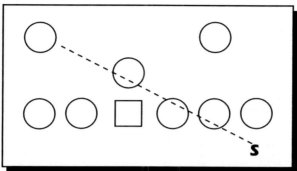

**Diagram 7.2**
**Sam linebacker split back key (cross key to the far back).**

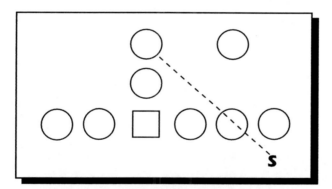

**Diagram 7.3**
**Sam linebacker strong back key  (cross key to the fullback).**

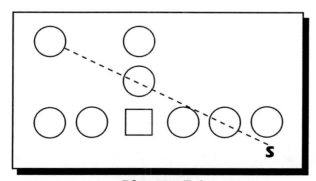

**Diagram 7.4**
**Sam linebacker weak back key (cross key to the halfback).**

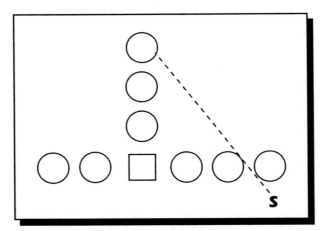

**Diagram 7.5**
**Sam linebacker I formation key (cross key to the tailback).**

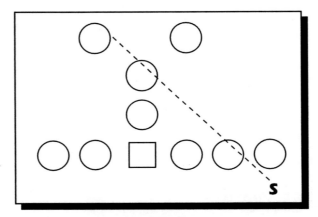

**Diagram 7.6**
**Sam linebacker wishbone formation key (cross key to the far back).**

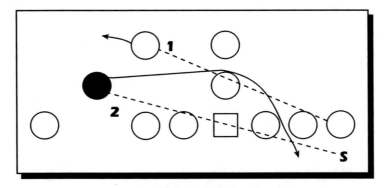

**Diagram 7.7**
**If the Sam linebacker reads the back going away from him,**
**he should cross key the slot or the wing for a trap or a counter play.**

If the Sam's back key goes away, Sam cross keys the slot or the wing and plays the trap or the counter (Diagram 7.7).

Versus an option play, Sam must trap the tight end on the line of scrimmage to keep him off the Mike linebacker.  Because Sam is responsible for the pitch back, he must take a path to the ball at approximately 45 degrees to contain it like a sweep (Diagram 7.8).  Although Sam usually has time to react, this play must be practiced, and the need for taking the proper pursuit course to the ball emphasized.

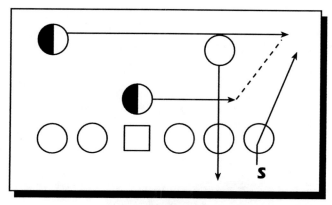

**Diagram 7.8**
**Sam linebacker responsibility vs. an option play.**

Versus a power play, the Sam linebacker must again trap the tight end on the line of scrimmage.  If the tight end attempts to hook Sam, Sam stays in the hole and attacks his formation key (Diagram 7.9).  If the tight end has Sam hooked, Sam stays on the line of scrimmage and makes a pile (Diagram 7.10).

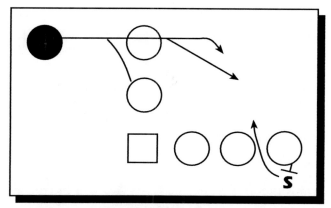

**Diagram 7.9**
**Sam linebacker vs. a power play.**

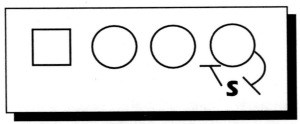

**Diagram 7.10**
**Sam linebacker vs. a hook block.**

Versus an isolation or sprint-draw play, Sam again traps the tight end and prevents him from taking an inside release on the inside linebackers. If the tight end blocks out on the end, Sam attacks the lead back, using his inside shoulder (Diagram 7.11). If the tight end hook blocks, Sam plays it like a power play.

Versus a quick toss or a sweep play, the tight end will normally release to the defensive end. Sam treats a sweep like a pitch on an option play. Sam contains such a play laterally, using a 45-degree pursuit course to the ball (Diagram 7.12).

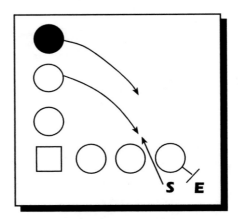

**Diagram 7.11**
**Sam linebacker vs. an isolation /sprint draw play.**

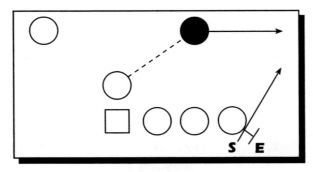

**Diagram 7.12**
**Sam linebacker vs. a quick toss/sweep play.**

Versus a trap play, it is again imperative that Sam keep the tight end off the inside linebackers. Sam cross keys his back and maintains his position on the line of scrimmage. He attacks the blocker or the running back with his inside shoulder, keeping his shoulders square. He maintains outside leverage with his outside shoulder, while preventing the back from bouncing the play outside (Diagram 7.13).

Versus a pass play, Sam has a flat drop in our base zone coverage, which we call green. The flat area is outside the widest receiver's position. We tell Sam to work to a depth of seven yards and stretch with the play if necessary (Diagram 7.14).

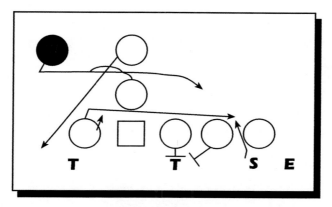

**Diagram 7.13**
**Sam linebacker vs. a trap play.**

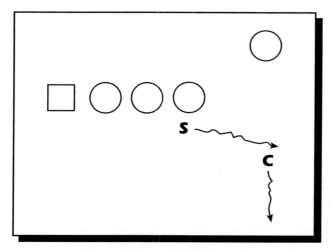

**Diagram 7.14**
**Sam linebacker's zone drop in a green**
**zone pass coverage.**

Against a slot formation with a lone tight end, the Sam can gang and allow the corner to help him.  If the full flow is away from him, there is no need for Sam to drop to the flat and cover grass (Diagram 7.15). Versus a screen or a draw play, Sam needs to study film and rely on his cross keys to react.

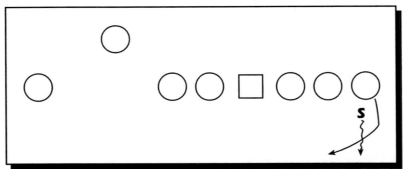

**Diagram 7.15**
**Sam linebacker vs. lone tight end.**

In man coverage, Sam generally takes the tight end versus the traditional formations, such as pro, slot, wide,  or twin.  Against a double-tight end formation, Sam takes the strongside tight end.  A complete breakdown of Sam's pass coverage responsibilities is presented in Appendix B (coverage responsibilities for linebackers and defensive backs in the split 4-4 defense).

### Rover Linebacker

The Rover is the weakside outside linebacker.  He can be either a true linebacker of a fourth defensive-back type.  He must be a versatile player because he is the player who is usually moved around in the split 4-4 defense.  Sam, on the other hand, usually stays over the tight end.  The Rover must be able to support on a run, defend against a pass, and also be a rush player.  This position is comparable to the strong safety or monster position in a 5-2 or a 3-4 alignment.

The Rover aligns in a two-point stance, protecting his outside foot.  His alignment against a split end/pro set is two-by-two, or two yards wide of the offensive tackle and two yards off the line of scrimmage (Diagram 7.16).  Rover has basically the same keys as the Sam linebacker. (Refer to diagrams 7.2 to 7.6).  He cross keys to the far back or to the tailback in the I formation.

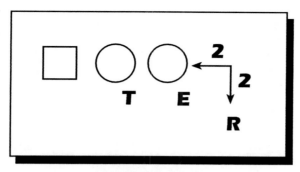

**Diagram 7.16**
**Rover alignment vs. a split end/pro set.**

A favorite strategy of offenses versus the split 4-4 is to attempt to split the Rover linebacker out with a wide slot alignment and to run the ball inside. Although we sometimes will adjust the Rover's alignment to the slot, it is a game-to-game strategic tactical decision. We are not going to remove Rover from a run-support position if the sole objective of the offense is to run the ball inside.

Versus a slot alignment, Rover will generally align at a depth of three yards, splitting the difference between a slot that is positioned out over five yards and the offensive tackle (Diagram 7.17). This extra depth allows Rover to cover width and discourages a quick pass to the slot.

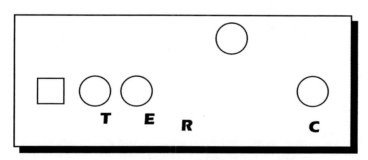

**Diagram 7.17**
**Rover alignment vs. a slot alignment.**

Versus slots who line up five yards or under from the offensive tackle, Rover will align on the slot's inside eye at a depth of three yards (Diagram 7.18). Versus a wide formation (i.e., a slot that lines up within two yards of a split end), Rover again splits the difference between the slot and the offensive tackle, at a depth of four yards (Diagram 7.19). As previously discussed, the additional depth helps Rover cover width.

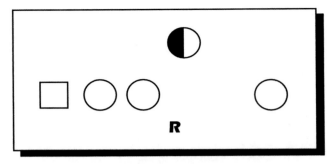

**Diagram 7.18**
**Rover alignment vs. a tight-slot alignment.**

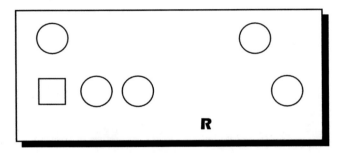

**Diagram 7.19**
**Rover alignment vs. a wide-slot formation.**

Emphasizing Rover's path to the ball, a team must practice against its opponent's slot formations and their companion running plays. The Rover must also be coached to read his keys, which will be at a different angle the farther out he is split. The Rover must remember that he is an outside linebacker with primary run responsibility. He may be prone to forget this factor from time to time because he is either generally loose on the weakside in a two-by-two alignment, or is split out versus a wide or twin formation. He must provide run support.

Versus the double wing/tight slot formation, the Rover plays a 8 technique two yards off the line of scrimmage (Diagram 7.20). Because this particular formation is balanced, the side Rover aligns on is dictated by an opponent's rushing tendencies as determined on the scouting report. Generally, the Rover will align on the weak-side of an opponent's rush tendency. Versus a trips formation, the Rover aligns on the inside eye of the #2 receiver (Diagram 7.21).

**Diagram 7.20**
**Rover alignment vs. a double-wing formation.**

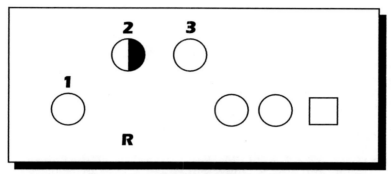

**Diagram 7.21**
**Rover alignment vs. a trips formation.**

The Rover is replaced by an extra defensive back in the nickel package.  The Rover could be bumped to the inside linebacker position as an alternative if the inside linebacker is a poor pass coverage player, or if an opponent's personnel dictates maximum coverage.  If the Rover is replaced by a fourth defensive back, a key coaching point is to make sure that the nickel defensive back understands that he must provide run support.  The nickel back should be run at in practice in order to become comfortable and proficient at supporting the run.

Versus an option play, the Rover cross keys to the far back and has pitch-back responsibility (Diagram 7.22).

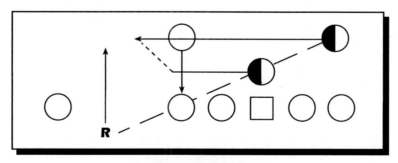

**Diagram 7.22**
**Rover responsibility on an option play.**

Versus a power play, the Rover attacks the ball carrier from outside in and maintains outside leverage (Diagram 7.23).

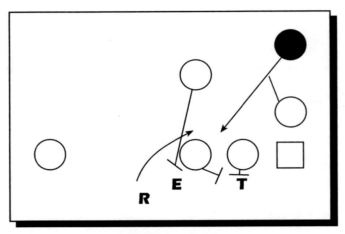

**Diagram 7.23**
**Rover vs. a power play.**

Versus an isolation play, the Rover attacks the ball carrier inside out (Diagram 7.24). Versus a counter or a trap play away, the Rover is in position to see it first (Diagram 7.25). Versus a counter or a trap play run toward him, the Rover is the extra man and attacks outside in (Diagram 7.26).

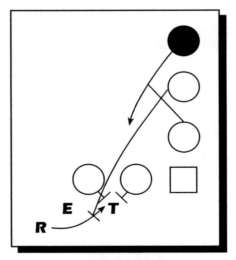

**Diagram 7.24**
**Rover vs. an isolation play.**

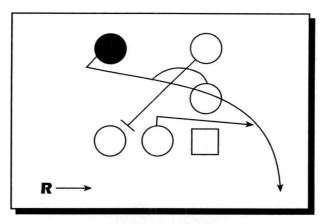

**Diagram 7.25**
**Rover vs. a counter/trap play away.**

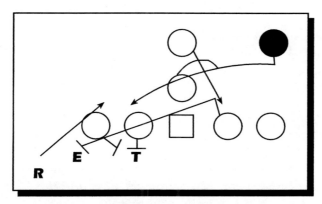

**Diagram 7.26**
**Rover vs. a counter/trap play run toward him.**

The coverage charts in the Appendix B present additional information on the responsibilities of the Rover for pass coverage.

# CHAPTER 8

# Secondary Play

### Cornerbacks

We predominantly employ a three-deep zone with our secondary. Although we have several man-to-man schemes which are necessary in our blitz package, we are basically a zone coverage team.

We always want to give the opponent's quarterback the same look regardless of the actual coverage we're in. We want to appear balanced, three straight up. We do not want to give the quarterback a pre-snap read. If we're going to cheat on the coverage, we'll move after the ball is snapped, not before.

Our cornerbacks are in a two-point stance with their inside foot up slightly. Our cornerbacks are positioned five yards off the line of scrimmage, aligned on the inside eye of the receiver. The corners never line up closer than five yards to the sideline. Because of our eight-man front and the inherent risk of the offensive breakaway play, the five-yard press alignment of our cornerbacks provides more efficient run support. At the snap of the ball, the cornerbacks execute a short shuffle to protect the inside of the field. They must take away the quick post first. All factors considered, a quick post is the easiest throw for the offense to make.

The cornerbacks' run support responsibility is a basic roll. If the ball comes to his side, he is a force player (Diagram. 8.1).

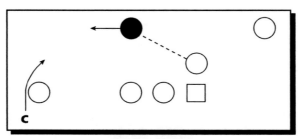

**Diagram 8.1**
**Cornerback play vs. a run action to him.**

If the ball goes away, the cornerback plays a half and takes a deep pursuit angle to the ball (Diagram 8.2). Versus an option play, the cornerback has pitch responsibility (Diagram 8.3).

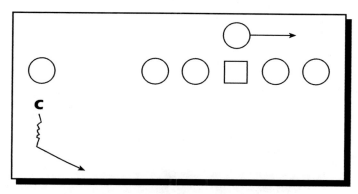

**Diagram 8.2**
**Cornerback pursuit angle vs. a run away from him.**

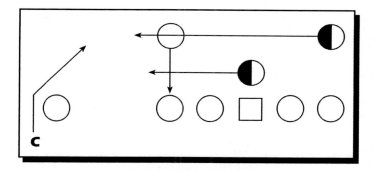

**Diagram 8.3**
**Cornerback vs. an option play.**

Versus a power or an isolation play, the cornerback fills from the outside in, maintaining outside leverage and guarding against an outside "bounce" by the ball carrier (Diagram 8.4).

Versus a reverse, the cornerback shuffles to half and squats, calling out "reverse". Immediate communication to the safety is crucial. From there, we want to reroll the zone towards the ball (Diagram 8.5). Appendix B provides additional information on the responsibilities of cornerbacks for run and pass coverage.

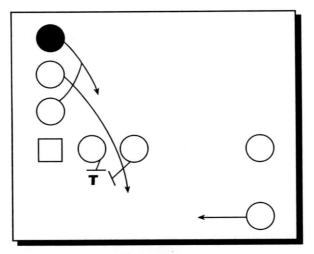

**Diagram 8.4**
**Cornerback play vs. an isolation/power play.**

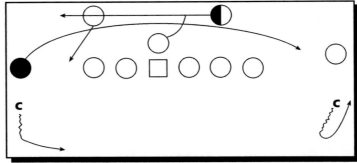

**Diagram 8.5**
**Cornerback play vs. a reverse.**

### The Safety

The name of the safety position signifies this player's main responsibilities. Because of the inherent risk of a breakaway play versus our eight-man front, the safety is largely responsible for keeping big plays (i.e., plays over forty yards) to a minimum. Accordingly, the safety must be an intelligent, sure-tackling defender who can follow directions and has a thorough understanding of the total defensive plan.

We operate out of a three-deep rolling zone concept in the secondary, with the safety rotating through the cornerback's position in run support (Diagram 8.6).

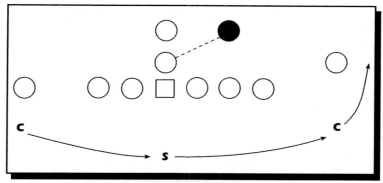

**Diagram 8.6**
**Safety run support rotation.**

We also play some man-free coverage, meaning the cornerbacks and linebackers have a specific man responsibility, while the safety is free to roam and help (Diagram 8.7). This particular defense takes specific advantage of the safety's requisite intelligence and "ball sense".

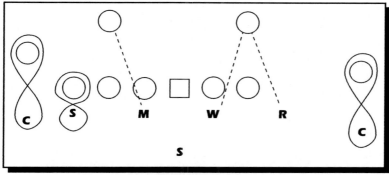

**Diagram 8.7**
**Man free coverage.**

The safety aligns in a two-point, square-shoulder stance, approximately eight yards off the ball in the middle of the offensive formation. We never want the safety aligned outside the guard on the multiple-receiver side, unless it is a trips formation, in which case he can adjust to being over the offensive tackle. We want the quarterback to always see the safety in the same place (i.e., middle) — pre-snap. We want the safety to appear to be "on top" of the formation. We may adjust the safeties depth according to down and distance or the pass/run frequency tendencies of the offense. We believe that 70% of the time, high school quarterbacks cannot read the secondary and have a predetermined receiver. The safety is just another body in the area.

Versus a trips set with the safety aligned over the offensive tackle, the Sam linebacker and the corner would have to banjo (i.e., work combination coverage) on the backside tight end and the running back (Diagram 8.8). Additional information on the run and pass responsibilities of the safety is presented in Appendix B.

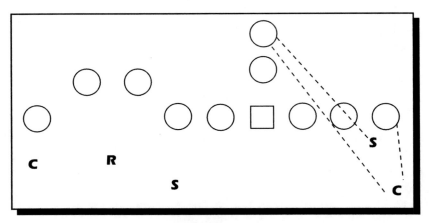

**Diagram 8.8**
**Trips formation coverage.**

# CHAPTER 9

# Pass Rush and Blitz Package

### Pass Rush

As the old axiom implies, the best pass defense is having the "best pass rush". Our pass rush in the split 4-4 defense is focused on having a plan. Our plan includes specific rush landmarks for the defensive tackles and ends who comprise the base four rushers. The tackles' landmark is the inside number of the quarterback to the particular end's side of the field. The ends' landmark is the quarterback's outside number to the particular end's side of the field (Diagram 9.1).

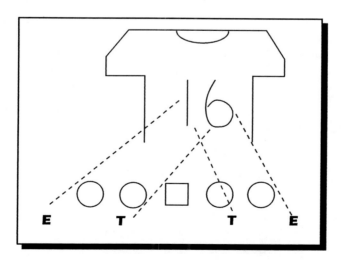

**Diagram 9.1**
**Rush landmarks for defensive tackles and ends.**

The major coaching points we always cover with our pass rushers include the following:

- Always try to maintain the game plan rush track.
- Never create escape lanes for the quarterback. Stay on track.
- If forced to an outside rush track, always think *underneath* the blocker to get back on track. This approach involves a crossover inside technique, generally using the offensive lineman's body position.
- Maintain assigned leverage for contain purposes.
- Remember that it often takes more that one move of a blocker to *escape*. Think of two or three moves you can employ. Change your technique regularly.
- Retrace your steps versus the draw play.

Each defensive position coach (and in turn each player) needs to understand the preparation necessary to execute an effective pass rush. That preparation begins with a careful study and evaluation of each of the offensive position players and how they perform their duties relative to the offensive scheme they're using.

In studying the opposition's quarterback, the following factors (relative to the quarterback's actions) must be considered:

- Where does he set up?
- Are there any changes in the speed of his steps per drop?
- Are there any changes in his style of running or the size of his steps?
- Are there changes in how he handles the ball per drop?
- What are his escape routes?
- Is he a risk taker?
- Will he reverse his field when confronted with stunts?
- How do his steps change when he is throwing a screen?
- Are there changes in his shoulder or his usual throwing motion when he's throwing a screen?
- What changes are there in his drop steps on a draw?
- Does the position he holds the ball in or his speed of operation change for a draw play?

In observing the opposition's running backs, the following points should be studied:

- Who do they block on all drops, stunts, screens, and draws?
- How do they set on a screen play and then get lost?
- Do they change their body position on a screen?
- Do they receive the ball differently on a draw?
- Are there any alignment changes or changes in the movement of the running back when running a draw?

When developing a pass rush plan, the following factors involving an opponent's receivers should be reviewed:

- Are their receivers involved in the screen game?
- Do these receivers tip off a screen play by their alignment or other different mannerisms?
- How do they get lost on a screen?

The most comprehensive, in-depth study should involve the opponent's offensive linemen and should address the following issues:

- What are the blocking schemes the offensive linemen use?
- Does the offensive line have weak areas which can be taken advantage of with stunts?
- How do they release and where do they set on a screen play?
- Which side of the offensive line, if any, blocks firm on a screen?
- What rush path does the offensive line want the defensive lineman to take on a draw?
- Do any of the offensive linemen change their body position or stance on a particular play?

Careful video evaluation that addresses all of the aforementioned factors can provide a team's defensive pass rushers with a substantial tactical advantage. These areas should be covered in a team's Monday meeting and worked on the field in seven-on-seven pass skeleton and defensive line walk throughs.


## Blitz Packages

An endless number of possibilities exist to create a comprehensive blitz package out of the split 4-4 defense. A few of the more successful blitz packages that we have used are discussed in the remainder of this chapter. Again, it should be emphasized that we want to play our base 40 defense as long as possible without having to blitz. Using front and coverage changes can be just as confusing to our opponents and their blocking schemes as blitzing. A coach should keep in mind that the split 4-4 is an unusual defensive front and that just blocking the base front all week generally involves a great deal of change in an opponent's blocking assignments. A coach should remember that the fourth criteria of successful defenses (discussed in chapter 1) is to create maximum confusion for the offense while keeping defensive instruction simple. This objective can sometimes be accomplished just by making alignment changes in response to a particular down-and-distance situation. While blitz packages can be an important component of the overall scheme in a split 4-4 defense, we try to keep the number of blitzes we employ to a minimum and to maximize our front changes.

*Sam/Rover Out*

The defensive ends work in unit with Sam and Rover. In this particular blitz package, the defensive end crashes, while the outside linebacker (Sam or Rover) loops to outside contain (Diagram 9.2). This is an excellent blitz versus option teams or flat-passing teams who operate out of a pro or an I formation.

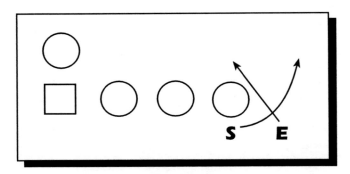

**Diagram 9.2**
**Sam/Rover out.**

*Sam/Rover Fire*

In this blitz package, Sam and Rover work as a team with the defensive ends. This blitz involves a straight stunt into the nearest inside gap by either Sam or Rover. The defensive end must concentrate on reading the play and on maintaining his outside leverage (Diagram 9.3). This blitz would typically be used either in a situation versus an off-tackle power play or an isolation play, or to create backside pressure.

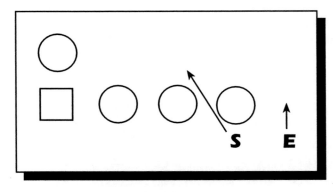

**Diagram 9.3**
**Sam/Rover fire.**

*Mike/Willie Fire*

In this blitz package, Mike and/or Willie team with the defensive tackle to their side. One or both linebackers blitz the A gap, while the defensive tackles control the B gap (Diagram 9.4). This stunt is relatively useless if the offense narrows its splits. In specific situations, it can be effective either against an isolation, a sprint draw/ power, or a trap/counter play, or as a pass blitz.

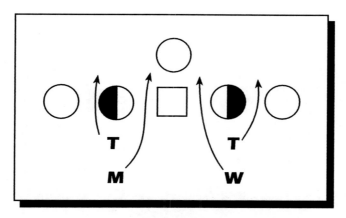

**Diagram 9.4**
**Mike/Willie fire.**

*Mike/Willie Baker*

In this blitz package, the defensive tackles slant to the A gap, taking the offensive guard. Mike or Willie fires through the B gap (Diagram 9.5). We use this stunt against a dive-option team, the power or sprint draw, or as a pass blitz.

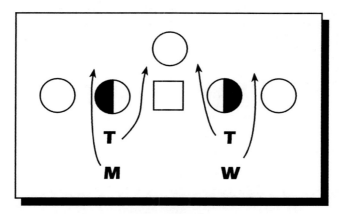

**Diagram 9.5**
**Mike/Willie baker.**

*Mike/Willie Loop*

In this blitz package, the defensive tackle loops in the direction called in the defensive huddle — either right or left.  The inside linebacker behind the looping tackle then fires through the A gap. The away tackle crosses the offensive guard's face to the A gap (Diagram 9.6). This stunt is used as a delayed pass blitz, usually with man/free coverage.

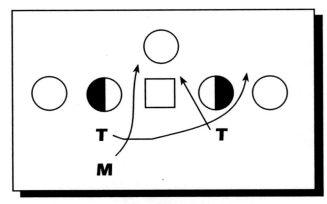

**Diagram 9.6**
**Mike/Willie loop.**

The aforementioned stunts and blitzes are most effective when they are used as infrequently employed change ups to normal rush patterns. The elements of surprise and suddenness are important factors in a successful defensive scheme.

# CHAPTER 10

# Making Defensive Adjustments

### Recognizing Formations

The split 4 - 4 is a variable defense that adjusts easily against various formations. During the course of a season, we will encounter several different offensive formations and backfield sets. Our terminology (name) for those formations is illustrated in Diagrams 10.1 to 10.11. It is important to have coaches and players on the same page with respect to terminology.

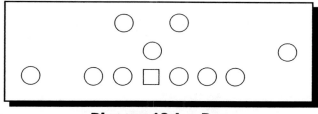

**Diagram 10.1 — Pro.**

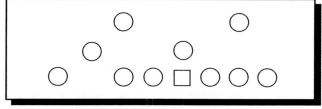

**Diagram 10.2 — Slot.**

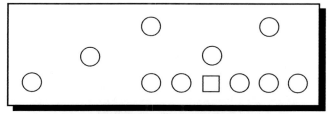

**Diagram 10.3 — Wide.**

Note: The flanker/slot splits the difference between the tackle and the split end on the three formations above.

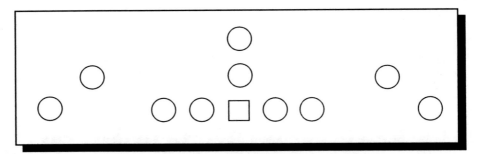

**Diagram 10.4 — Twin.**

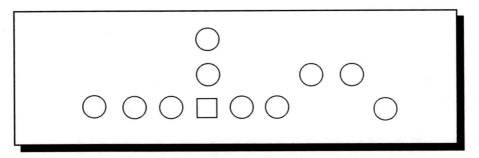

**Diagram 10.5 — Trips.**

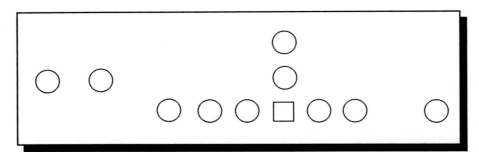

**Diagram 10.6 — TE Trips.**

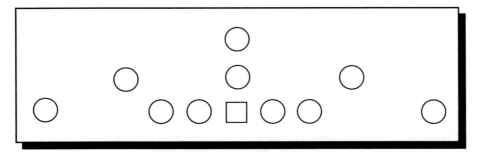

**Diagram 10.7 — Wing.**

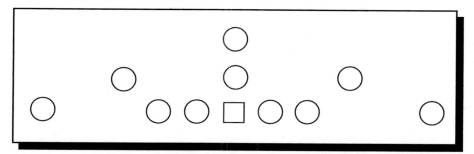

**Diagram 10.8 — Double Wing.**

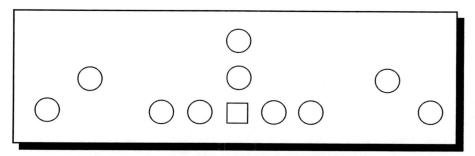

**Diagram 10.9 — Double Twin.**

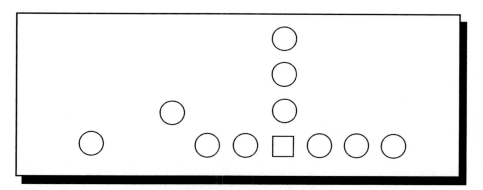

**Diagram 10.10 — Tight Slot.**

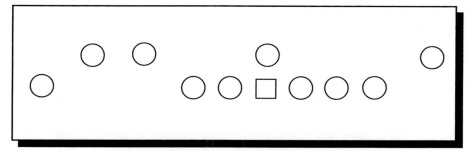

**Diagram 10.11 — Trips Left Pro Right.**

## Backfield Sets

We also face a variety of backfield sets over the course of the season. Each particular type of set and our terminology for that set is illustrated in Diagrams 10.12 to 10.19.

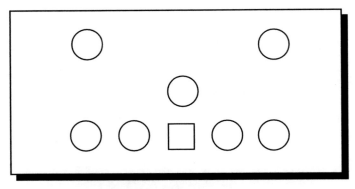

**Diagram 10.12 — Split.**

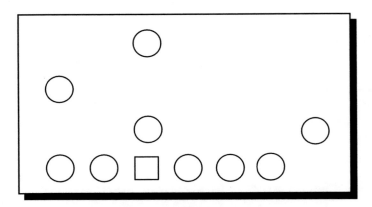

**Diagram 10.13 — Weak.**

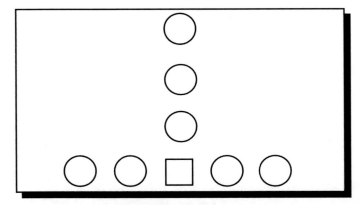

**Diagram 10.14 — I.**

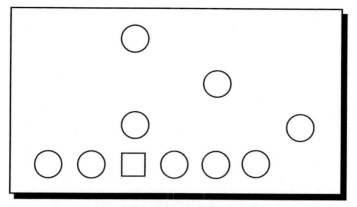

**Diagram 10.15 — Strong.**

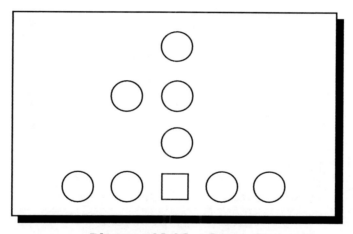

**Diagram 10.16 — Power I.**

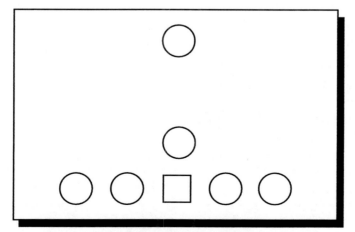

**Diagram 10.17 — Ace.**

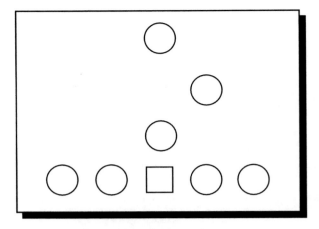

**Diagram 10.18 — I Bone.**

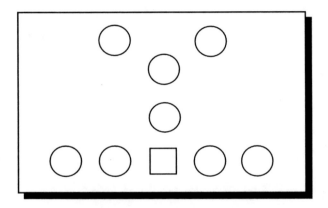

**Diagram 10.19 — Bone.**
**(If bone is broken, we still treat as a bone).**

### Motion Adjustments

Our philosophy regarding how to react to motion by the offense is that such motion simply changes the formation. We align on formation and bump defenders over in response to motion. As the motion man goes toward the ball and passes receivers or backs, we readjust according to our front call (Diagram 10.20). Some fronts will be wiped (changed) depending on motion frequency.

If the defense is in man-to-man coverage, communication between defensive players is a must. If an offensive man goes in motion, his defender must signal to the next defender to take him (Diagram 10.21). The defender to whom the signal was directed should then give his teammate an acknowledgment that he received the signal so that everyone is clear on the need for an adjustment.

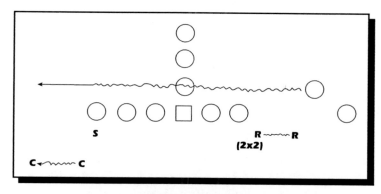

**Diagram 10.20**
**Motion adjustment (twin to pro).**

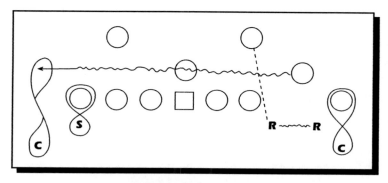

**Diagram 10.21**
**Motion vs. man-to-man coverage.**

If a running back goes in motion, Mike and Willie pass him quickly to the corner. The formation is now simply a pro formation to the corner's side (Diagram 10.22). If a defense is in man-to-man coverage, when the back passes the tight end, he becomes the corner's man(Diagram 10.23). Again, communication is the key.

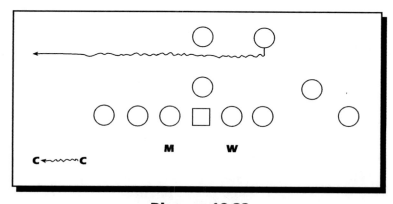

**Diagram 10.22**
**Back motion vs. zone coverage.**

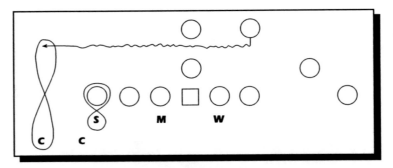

**Diagram 10.23**
**Back motion vs. man-to-man coverage.**

If motion overloads a formation (such as a tight-end shift), Sam would walk off to a two-by-two position. A coach should remember that Sam and Rover are technically interchangeable. Rover would widen the end and step up (Diagram 10.24). The corners and safety must communicate with the linebackers and one another about who is and isn't on the line of scrimmage.

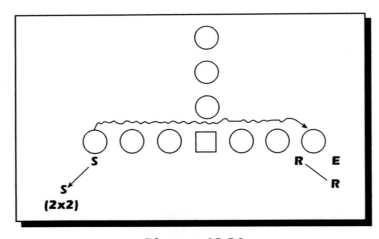

**Diagram 10.24**
**Motion adjustment vs. a tight-end shift.**

Versus split and motion to overload, Rover would bump to stack on the defensive tackle. Willie would bump to Mike's spot. Mike would bump to stack on Sam (Diagram 10.25). Because this is a difficult situation, it must be practiced and chalked repeatedly. A note of caution: the offense can still run weak or counter isolation to keep a team honest.

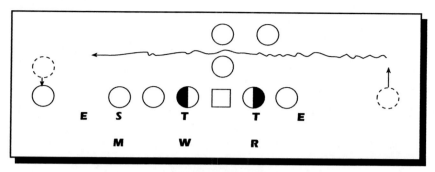

**Diagram 10.25**
**Motion adjustment vs. split end motion to overload.**

## Special Formation Adjustments

When confronting an unbalanced formation, we move our front over towards the strong-side (Diagram 10.26). We treat the center as a weakside 3 technique. We move the strongside defensive tackle to a 6 technique. Willie shifts to the A gap weakside, and Mike shifts to the B gap strongside. All responsibilities remain the same.

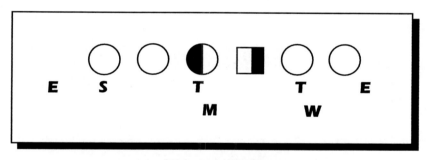

**Diagram 10.26**
**Adjustment to an unbalanced formation.**

When facing an unbalanced formation, all fronts are wiped except the "50". In the 50 front, the weakside defensive tackle plays on the center in a 3 technique. Willie gets in a three-point stance in a 3 technique on the strongside guard and blitzes the B gap. The strongside defensive tackle plays the C gap. All the remaining linebackers, Rover, Mike, and Sam, stack and maintain three to four yards of depth for proper reading angles (Diagram 10.27).

The only time we would stay in the 50 front versus the unbalanced formation is against a power/isolation team when penetration was necessary, and then only on first down or a second-and-long situation. We return to our base defense on any third-down situation.

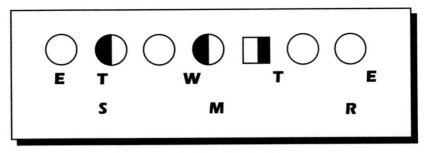

**Diagram 10.27**
**50 front vs. an unbalanced formation.**

A formation we see often is the tight slot alignment (Diagram 10.28). This formation can cause problems because of the blocking leverage positions of the slot personnel. The split end has approximately a four-yard split, while the flanker or slot splits the difference between the split end and the offensive tackle.

From a tight slot formation, the offense is capable of running a myriad of plays, including power, isolation, sweep, quick toss, screen, and option. The secondary must give quick run support, but must also be aware of the possibility of a pass. Mike and Willie have to play no closer than five yards to the line of scrimmage. They need to get depth to cover width. Teams that utilize the tight-slot formation generally create the tight slot away from a team's bench so it is more difficult for a defensive team to detect. A team which positions a spotter in the press box must be sure that the spotter has an agenda and is aware of this formation.

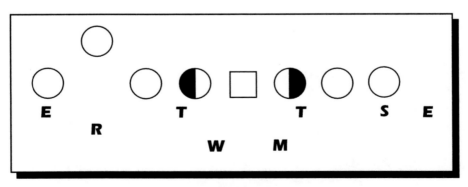

**Diagram 10.28**
**Alignment vs. a tight-slot formation.**

## The Defensive Huddle

Our defensive huddle is formed as illustrated in Diagram 10.29. Mike generally calls the signals. Sam and Rover are situated in the middle of the huddle so they can break either way.

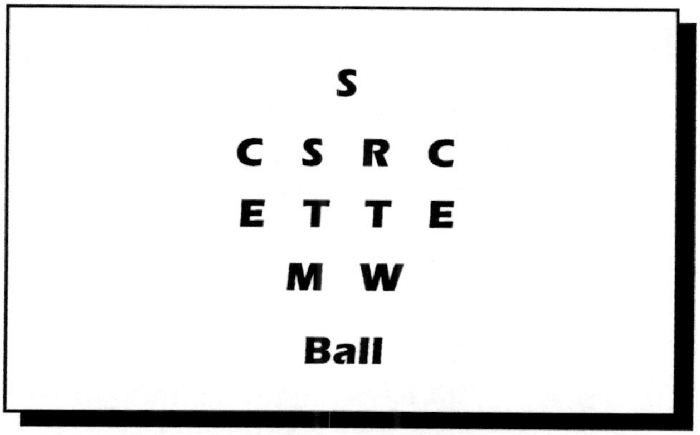

```
              S

      C   S   R   C

      E   T   T   E

          M   W

         Ball
```

**Diagram 10.29**
**The defensive huddle.**

# CHAPTER 11

# Drills for the Split 4-4 Defense

### DRILL #1: TRAP DRILL

*Objective:*  To teach defensive tackles the proper techniques involved in squeezing a trap play.

*Equipment Needed:*  None.

*Description:*  The drill involves five players—two defensive tackles (DTs) and three offensive linemen (two guards and a center).  The DTs lineup in their 3 technique. One offensive guard is designated as a pulling guard, while the center and the other guard are assigned to clear block an inside linebacker.  The drill begins on the command of the coach to "trap right" or "trap left", which is  a signal to the left or the right guard to trap.  The DT over the pulling guard puts his hand on the pulling guard's hip and follows him.  The DT that is being released drops to all fours, squares his shoulders, and attempts to attack the trapper with his inside shoulder.  The drill is conducted at half-speed (never live).  Once a team has performed several repetitions of the drill, the coach can designate one or more relatively small groups to perform the drill.  The players rotate themselves through the drill in order to get more repetitions and to minimize the amount of time they have to stand around.

*Coaching Points:*

- DT's should maintain a square-shoulders position.
- The DT should attack the trap blocker before the blocker attacks him.
- The DT should maintain outside leverage with his free hand and leg.
- This drill should be conducted at least one period every week.

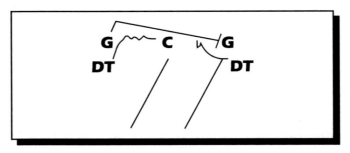

**Diagram 11.1**
**Drill #1**

## DRILL #2: PATHS TO THE BALL

*Objective:*  To enhance the ability of outside linebackers to recognize and react to their proper keys; to practice taking the proper pursuit angles to the ball carrier; to improve footwork.

*Equipment Needed:*  A football; five cones.

*Description:*  This drill is conducted in two phases.  In both phases, the coach serves as the quarterback.  In the first phase, the coach sets three cones in line to serve as offensive linemen.  He also sets two cones approximately 4-5 yards apart in the backfield to signify where the ball would be if particular plays were being run. The drill involves one outside linebacker (OLB) at a time who assumes a position over the (offensive lineman) cone at his far left.  The coach/quarterback lines up behind the cone to the OLB's far right.  The drill begins on the coach's command ("go").  The coach then either opens up and simulates running an option play or reverses out and simulates running an iso/power/trap/counter play.  The OLB takes a read step and delivers a blow against air.  He then reacts to the actions of the coach/quarterback.  He attacks the area (cone) designated by the play the coach/ quarterback is running.   The first phase is conducted at half-speed versus no opposition (air).  In the second phase, ball carriers (aligned in the backfield) and a tight end are added.  The tight end works on trap stepping.  The drill is now conducted full speed on the line and then thump to the ball. (Note: "thump or "thud" is a term which refers to a situation when there is initial contact but no tackling).  Later on, the sequence is thump and then live once the OLB finds the right area.

*Coaching Points:*

*   Taking the proper track to attack the ball should be emphasized.
*   The importance of using and maintaining the proper stance, body positioning , feet movement, and hand placement should be stressed.
*   OLB's should be made aware of their responsibilities on certain plays and where help will be given to them.
*   OLB's must develop the ability to read and react to their backfield keys.

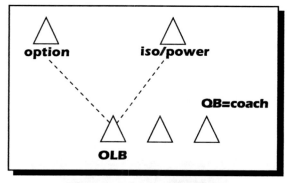

**Diagram 11.2 — Drill #2**

## DRILL #3: MIKE/WILLIE
## PURSUIT/PATH TO THE BALL

*Objective:* To enhance the ability of inside linebackers to take the proper pursuit angle to the ball; to recognize and react to backfield keys; to practice taking on blocks, using the proper shoulder; to improve the ability of defenders to provide backside support; to develop footwork.

*Equipment Needed:* Four blocking dummies; a football.

*Description:* This drill is conducted in three phases. In all three phases, the coach acts as the quarterback. The four blocking dummies are spaced out to serve as four offensive linemen—two on each side of the ball. The two inside linebackers (Mike and Willie) are aligned as they would be in a 40 base defense. The first phase of the drill is conducted at half-speed, thump (i.e., contact but no tackling) to the ball. On the coach's command, the quarterback/coach drops one step and then moves laterally down the line to his right. Both inside linebackers (ILB) then take a read step. The onside ILB (Mike) crosses over and prepares to take on an offensive block with his inside shoulder. When he arrives at the point of attack, he squares up in the hole. The backside ILB (Willie), having taken a read step, drops his butt and does not cross the midline until the ball has crossed the line of scrimmage (i.e., he maintains backside support). In this phase, the drill is conducted versus air until the ILB's have perfected their footwork and have gained the confidence to get to the point of attack. In phase #2, offensive linemen are added to the drill. The drill is then conducted live on the line thump to the ball. The key is to practice having the ILB's get off their blocks. Phase #3 is conducted just as phase #2, except that the drill is conducted 100% live.

*Coaching Points:*

- ILB's should maintain a depth of 4-5 yards.
- ILB's should take a read step on every play.
- ILB's should use the proper shoulder when escaping from a block.
- ILB's should develop the ability to recognize and react to their backfield keys.
- ILB's should learn where they have and don't have help on a play.

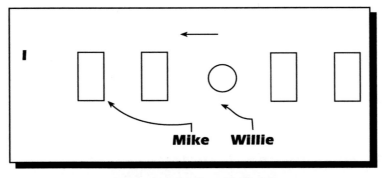

**Diagram 11.3 — Drill #3**

## DRILL #4: SQUARE CORNER DRILL

*Objective:*  To teach defensive tackles to stay down on a trap block and to keep their heads up (field) while being blocked.

*Equipment Needed:*  None.

*Description:*  This drill is conducted in two phases.  In both phases, the coach stands behind the defensive tackle (DT), who is positioned straight ahead on all fours.  The rest of the DTs (or offensive linemen if the coach chooses) are divided into two groups.  The two groups are lined up 4-5 yards from the DT who is participating in the drill at a right angle to the DT.  Phase #1 of the drill begins when the coach points to one of the lines.  The player who has been pointed at gently goes down the line to block the DT and thumps the DT, simulating a trap block. The DT lines his shoulder up with the imaginary line between him and the group the blocker came from and takes on the blocker with the shoulder nearest the blocker.  The DT keeps his head up field and his shoulders square, and uses the imaginary line as his guide.  He performs 4-6 repetitions of the drill before the players rotate, and a new DT participates.  In phase #2, the drill is conducted live. The coach should make sure that players are not exposed to an undue chance of being injured.  For example, experienced players should not work against inexperienced players.  In addition, players should be reminded not to intentionally attempt to injure anyone.  In this phase, the number of repetitions a DT performs is reduced to 2-3 before a new DT rotates into the drill.

*Coaching Points:*

- Unless a specific need exists (i.e., a coach is having difficulty keeping his DT's down), this drill need not be performed after the first two weeks of the regular season.
- Until players become proficient at this drill, the players should walk through the drill in order to minimize the chances of injury.
- A DT should keep his head upfield and his shoulders square with the imaginary line.
- A DT should maintain outside leverage with his opposite hand when a ball carrier bounces out off of a squeezed trap block.
- If offensive blockers are used in this drill, they should understand that they are working on their trap blocking technique, not trying to blow up the DT.

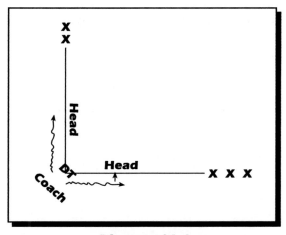

**Diagram 11.4**
**Drill #4**

## DRILL #5: DOUBLE TEAM DRILL

*Objective:* To enhance the ability of a defensive tackle to hold up a double team block, to avoid being combo clocked, and to maintain his position on the line of scrimmage.

*Equipment Needed:* None.

*Description:* This drill is conducted in two phases. Both phases are the same except that the first phase is conducted at half-speed, while the second phase is performed at full speed. The drill involves three players at a time—two offensive blockers (a post man and a drive man) and a defensive tackle (DT). The DT assumes a 3 technique, while the two blockers lineup opposite the DT. On a signal from the coach, the post man attempts to block the DT. As the DT "feels the double team," he butt rolls to the drive man. The DT collapses his inside knee. He then attempts to get his feet planted firmly and his hands down. He then pushes back into the double team—especially the drive man. As the DT pushes, he tries to maintain his position on the line of scrimmage. The DT does not want to get moved upfield. After the DT has stopped the motion of the blockers, he rolls into the hole.

*Coaching Points:*

- If a coach uses actual offensive linemen in the drill (instead of simply rotating three DTs into the various roles), it is important for the offensive linemen to realize that they are working on enhancing their skills, as well as the DT is working on his.
- Conducting the drill at half-speed enables players to learn the various skills involved in the drill and feel safe and secure while doing it.
- The need for the DT to maintain his position on the line of scrimmage should be emphasized.
- DTs should stay down while being blocked (i.e., they should never stand up); they should collapse immediately upon contact when being double-team blocked.
- Safety should be stressed.

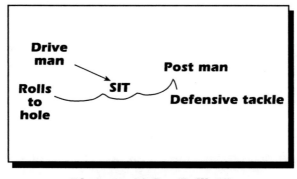

**Diagram 11.5 — Drill #5**

## DRILL #6: PASS RUSH LATERAL PURSUIT

*Objective:* To enhance the ability a defensive tackle or end to shed a blocker and to keep moving; to develop a never-quit attitude; to practice letting the secondary know it's a pass play.

*Equipment Needed:* Six blocking dummies.

*Description:* The drill involves two players—an offensive blocker and a defensive lineman (an end or a tackle). Five of the dummies are spaced side-by-side in a line, approximately 2-3 yards apart. The sixth blocking dummy is positioned upright 5-7 yards behind the line of five dummies. This dummy is designated as the "quarterback". Starting in a two-point stance facing each other, the blocker on one side of the line of dummies, the defender positioned in the middle of the dummies, both players move laterally down the line. As they move, the blocker attempts to hold the defender so that the defender can learn to deal with being held. Using his hands to free himself, the defender continues to move laterally to his left, by stepping over the dummies on the ground. The blocker mirrors the lateral progress of the defender. When both players reach the end of the line of dummies, the offensive lineman attempts to block the defender. The defender uses whatever defensive technique is appropriate to escape from the block. He then sprints (under control) and tackles the upright dummy (quarterback). As he runs toward the quarterback, he yells pass continuously.

*Coaching Points:*

- Proper footwork should be emphasized.
- The defender should maintain the proper body position while moving. His hips should be low and his knees bent.
- The defender should practice a variety of techniques to escape the block.
- The need to communicate to the secondary that it's a pass play should be stressed.

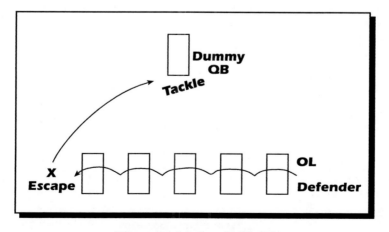

**Diagram 11.6 — Drill #6**

## DRILL #7: PASS RUSH AGAINST TWO BLOCKERS

*Objective:* To improve the ability of a defender to defeat two separate blocks while rushing the passer; to practice taking the proper path (angle) to the quarterback while pass rushing.

*Equipment needed:* Four blocking dummies.

*Description:* The drill initially involves three players—an offensive lineman (OL) and a defender (who begins the drill in the same positions as they were in Drill #6) and a running back. Three of the blocking dummies are laid on line adjacent to each other 1-2 yards apart. The fourth blocking dummy is positioned (upright) approximately 3-4 yards behind the running back who is lined up 3-4 yards diagonally from the blocking dummy which is furthest on the left. Similar to drill #6, the drill begins on a command from the coach. The defender moves laterally to his left, stepping over the three blocking dummies. The OL, mirroring the defender's movements, attempts to hold the defender while he is moving. When the defender clears the last blocking dummy, he uses an escape technique to get by the OL who is attempting to block him. Almost immediately after he has gotten by the OL, the defender must take on another block—this time by the running back. Again, the defender must counter the offensive block. The defender must get his inside leverage hand inside the running back's hands and arms in order to be able to control him. Once by the running back, the defender takes a straight path to the upright blocking dummy (that signifies a stationary quarterback) and tackles it. As he runs toward the imaginary quarterback, the defender should yell "pass".

*Coaching Points:*

- The need for the defender to take a straight path to the quarterback while pass rushing should be emphasized.
- The importance of the defender using his hands properly to counter the efforts of the running back to block him should be stressed.
- The defender should vary the moves he uses to escape attempts to block him.
- The defender should signal the defensive backs that it is a pass play by loudly yelling "pass" as he moves towards the quarterback.
- Once the defender has generally mastered his pass rushing techniques, the coach can replace the blocking dummy serving as a quarterback with a "live" quarterback.

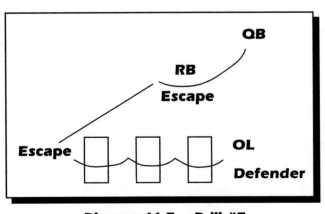

**Diagram 11.7 — Drill #7**

## DRILL #8:  REACTING TO THE QUARTERBACK

*Objective:*  To improve the ability of a defensive end to recognize the play because of the quarterback's motion and to react accordingly.

*Equipment Needed:*  Three cones.

*Description:*  The drill involves one defensive end (DE) and the coach, who serves as the quarterback (QB).  The three cones are placed in a straight line, 1-2 yards apart, as designated offensive linemen (i.e., one side of an offensive line).  The DE and QB assume their regular positions.  The drill begins on the movement of the QB.  The DE takes a read step every time.  If the QB opens with his numbers toward the DE, the DE reads the option and tries to attack at the B gap, while keeping his head upfield.  On the other hand, if the quarterback reverses out, the DE keys the near back. He then squeezes the power or ISO play, contains on a sweep, and trails as deep as the deepest back on a reverse/counter play.

Coaching Points:

* The need for the DE to take a read step and maintain outside leverage should be emphasized.
* One of the primary objectives of a DE is to make the field "smaller."
* The DE should attack an option play hard and fast.
* The DE should *never go inside.*
* The DE should maintain backside leverage to protect against a counter or a reverse play.

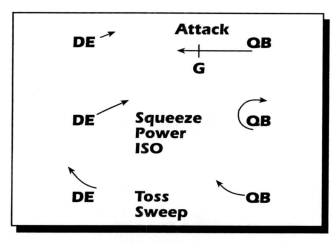

**Diagram 11.8**
**Drill #8**

### DRILL #9: INSIDE COORDINATED ATTACK

*Objective:* To improve the ability of the defensive tackles and the two inside linebackers to coordinate their efforts to defend against running plays in the middle of the line.

*Equipment Needed:* A football.

*Description:* This drill involves four defenders (two defensive tackles and the two inside linebackers—Mike and Willie) and six offensive players (a full backfield and three offensive linemen—the center and both guards). Based upon information provided by the scouting report, the offensive players run all of the inside running plays their opponent usually runs, including off-tackle plays. The three most widely run plays are highlighted. The four defensive players react to their keys, recognize the blocking schemes being employed, avoid the blocks, and attack the ball. For the first 5-10 minutes, this drill is conducted on a walk-through basis so that all of the players can get a feel for what the drill involves. After that, the drill is conducted at half-speed.

*Coaching Points:*

- The need for defenders to recognize and use the proper path (track) to attack the ball should be emphasized.
- Defenders should read their keys.
- Defenders should recognize the blocking schemes being used.
- The importance for defenders to maintain backside leverage should be stressed.
- The coach should ensure that each defender is aware of where help will come from—if any.

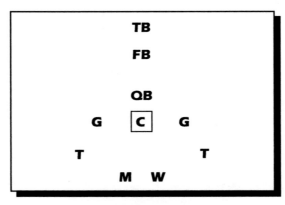

**Diagram 11.9**
**Drill #9**

## DRILL #10:  OUTSIDE COORDINATED ATTACK

*Objective:*  To improve the ability of the defensive ends and two outside linebackers to coordinate their efforts to defend against running plays to the outside.

*Equipment Needed:*  A football.

*Description:*  The drill involves four defenders (two defensive ends and the two outside linebackers) and an entire offensive team.  Based upon information provided by the scouting report, the offensive team runs all of the outside running plays their opponent usually runs—with particular emphasis on their opponent's three favorite running plays to the outside.  The four defenders react to their keys, recognize the blocking schemes being employed, avoid the blocks and attack the ball.  For the first 5-10 minutes, this drill is conducted on a walk-through basis so that all of the players can get a feel for what the drill involves.  After that, the drill is conducted at half-speed.

*Coaching Points:*

- The need for defenders to recognize and use the proper path (track) to attack the ball should be emphasized.
- Defenders should read their keys.
- Defenders should recognize the blocking schemes being used.
- The importance for defenders to maintain backside leverage should be stressed.
- The coach should ensure that each defender is aware of where help will come from—if any.

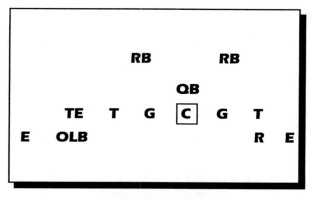

**Diagram 11.10**
**Drill #10**

# CHAPTER 12

# Game Preparation

## The Scouting Report

The essential element of all great football schemes is preparation. All of our defensive schemes are developed according to the formation, down and distance, hashmark, and area-of-the-field tendencies of our opponent. How our personnel match up with our opponent's is also a major consideration.

We use a computer scout system to clearly break down all of our scouting materials. Earlier in my career we did this by hand, which caused it to be a four-to-eight hour process. Computers have sped up this process considerably. A coach must be designated to program the scouting report in the computer in order to ensure that the computer breakdown of a particular game is in the staff's hands by Tuesday morning (following the game) at the latest.

In order to properly prepare for an opponent, a thorough and comprehensive scouting report of that team is necessary. We typically assign scouting duties to our freshman coaches. Some schools hire ex-coaches to scout. The scouting assignment should identify one coach as being responsible for the writeup of material for entry into the computer, and for a general summary of information to be presented at the meeting and the Monday players' meeting.

At a minimum, the scouting report should contain the following items:

- Down-and-distance information.
- Hash-mark and field-position tendencies (60% of the game is played on the hash).
- Any general glaring tendencies.
- All offensive information, including backfield and receiver alignments.

- All rushing plays. (If the scouts can pick up the blocking schemes, all the better. However, the opponent's blocking schemes against us are likely to be different because of our use of the split 4 - 4 defense).
- Yardage gained on specific plays.
- Any touchdowns.
- All passing plays, including alignments and routes, completions, incompletions, yardage, and touchdowns.

After the breakdown of the scouting report material, a coach must make decisions regarding what situational-front alignment and coverage changes are needed for the upcoming week. For example, we may incorporate some stunts into a particular week's defensive package, depending on the situation. Furthermore, personnel changes may be necessary to place the proper players in position for any alignment or coverage changes. At times, we may have a need to "hide" a weaker defender, again depending on the situation. We may also decide that we do not want certain players in the game situationally dictated by down and distance, field position, or time remaining to be played.

In addition to scouting opponents, we also exchange video of previous games with our opponents. We generally get one game we have seen and another game we haven't seen. The defensive coordinator breaks down the game we haven't scouted, using the same procedure as an actual scout. We generally make two copies of each tape, one for the offensive staff and another for the defensive staff. In reality, however, we'll make as many copies as necessary to accommodate our needs. On Monday through Thursday, all of our defensive players meet at lunch to review the tapes. They all have their scouting reports with them and are encouraged to take notes. On Fridays, we have a general meeting during which all defensive, offensive, and kicking information is reviewed.

## Preparing the Defensive Plan

In preparing the defensive game plan, we base our decisions about our defensive scheme on the following information about our opponent (which is developed through analyzing the  scouting tendencies):

- Their three best inside running plays
- Their three best outside running plays
- Their three best short passes
- Their three best long passes
- Any trick plays

We generally develop three possible fronts and coverages to deal with each of those 12 plays. By limiting our focus to 12 plays plus any trick plays, we are able to run most drills off of a play script.

We operate on the philosophy that while it can be very difficult to stymie all that the opponent does, what an opponent does well offensively must be stopped. A coach should make his opponent change to beat his team. Sometimes forcing an opponent to change what it likes to do is viewed as a victory in and of itself. As a general rule, high school coaches are creatures of habit, and will most often repeat previously successful plays. This circumstance is especially true after a turnover, at the beginning of a game, or in a clutch situation.

Just as we attempt to get our opponent's offense out of its comfort zone, we must have an adjustment plan for ourselves defensively if our opponent is getting the best of us. A coach must base this plan on an opponent's scouting frequencies. A coach should script situations he does not want his team to be in and develop and practice a plan to cope with those game situations. A coach should always be prepared for the worst case scenario. Sometimes the best and simplest adjustment is to go back to base split 4 - 4 defense, and just play football. The confidence of the defensive unit must not be shaken. The defensive unit must be confident and aggressive in the base defense. A coaching staff must have confidence that its base defense can stop anything.

## Practice Organization

During the preseason, we do not begin to practice defensively until the third or fourth practice. We concentrate on offense for the first three practices because the offense is generally behind developmentally. Even though we are not performing defensive drills, we are blocking our split 4-4 defense. Essentially, we are coaching both sides of the ball.

### Mondays

During the season, Monday is the day we begin to implement the game plan. The day begins with a 5:30 a.m. staff meeting. Monday afternoon's practice emphasis is primarily offense and kicking. After practice, we have a varsity team meeting where basic information contained in a written scouting report is given to each player. Each player is responsible for the information. Concurrently, we have a question-and-answer period during the meeting regarding our opponent. Each position coach must review the current opponent's video so that each coach is familiar with our opponent's schemes and can address questions from his group of players.

On Monday evening, the coaches meet and make decisions on all our fronts and coverages based on the opponent's tendencies, relative to down and distance, field position, formation, and hash mark. We discuss the requisite changes that might be necessary. We review any trick plays, and questions are answered by the position coaches. At the conclusion of the meeting, the head coach gives his final approval of the defensive game plan.

*Tuesdays*

Tuesday's defensive practice is organized into six major periods: individual, combo, thunder, seven-on-seven, goal line, and pride.

- Individual period. The "individual period" is organized into three, five-minute periods. During the preseason, we work on alignment, stance, basic responsibilities, and tackling. Care must be taken to conduct drills that are relevant to the skills that will actually be used in play, and not to drill just for the sake of drilling. Drills should have a specific purpose to teach a specific skill. During the season, drills and skill development should focus on the specific needs attendant to playing our particular opponent that week, or on reinforcing fundamental skills learned in the preseason. Talking on the field should be kept to a minimum. Coaches should keep players moving, giving them a maximum number of repetitions.

- Combo period. Like the individual period, the "combo period" is organized into three, five-minute periods. It is called the combo period because Sam and Rover are combined or paired with the defensive ends, while Mike and Willie are paired with the defensive tackles. During this period, the defensive backs remain separate and conduct an extended individual period. The defensive backs will get their walk-throughs during the thunder period. The front eight are given a walk-through of the opponent's run attack in each player's specific area. We show the players the most likely blocking schemes they will face. We then have a question-and-answer period. The position coach must be prepared to cover the necessary information.

- Thunder period. The "thunder period" is a run-through period, in which no defensive backs are involved. Players go through their walk-throughs during this time. In the thunder period, ten offensive players go against eight defenders. It is a scripted period in which we run the opponent's best inside and outside running plays, plus any trick plays our opponent might employ, like reverses.

- Seven-on-seven period. The "seven-on-seven period" begins with a basic walk through of our opponent's best pass plays, involving all of the linebackers and defensive backs. We then run a pass skeleton drill, throwing our opponent's pass plays against our defense. During this period, the defensive line is given a pass-rush period to work on schemes, landmarks and rush lanes to the quarterback, and their basic techniques. The defensive line also works on screen and draw plays. This time is an important period for the defensive line, since an effective pass rush is the primary component of a successful pass defense.

- Goal-line period. The "goal line period" is a  scripted walk-through of our defensive scheme versus the opponent's goal line offense. Any accompanying personnel changes are dealt with in this period.

- Pride period. The "pride period" is a full eleven-on-eleven team defensive period which is organized into five, five-minute periods. The opponent's plays are scripted and run against our full defense according to information provided by our opponent's scouting frequencies. We try to simulate the same run/pass ratio we have from our scouting report. We want to be thorough and leave nothing to chance. We use color coding to match the scout team's play cards with the scout team coaches' script.

### Wednesday

We practice offense, defense, and special teams on Wednesdays. The defensive part of practice is organized as follows:

- Combo period. On Wednesday, the "combo period" is organized into three, five - minute periods, with the defensive line working on pass rushing and the sled. The linebackers and defensive backs have a scripted seven-on-seven period.
- Goal-line period. Wednesday's "goal-line period" is split into two, five-minute scripted periods.
- Pride period. The "pride period" on Wednesday is five, five-minute periods, or until we are finished. If we have to go longer, we do. It is a scripted review of the plays that gave the defense trouble on Tuesday, or any additional plays not seen by the defense on Tuesday.

### Thursday

Thursday is generally a day in which we emphasize the offensive and kicking game. This practice usually lasts about an hour and 45 minutes. We only practice defensively, if it is absolutely necessary. Philosophically, we like to rest the defense on Thursdays, thinking that "hungry dogs hunt best" on Friday nights! We have a 5:30 p.m. staff dinner meeting and a 7:00 p.m. team meeting at a player's house.

### Friday

On Friday, we have a noon team meeting to review the scouting report, review all teams and personnel, and cover any general information necessary before the game.

## Game Coaching

I like to meet and chalk with our defense after every series. A critical tool is the defensive game script that I have an assistant coach keep on the sideline during the game. Adjustments that need to be made during the game with defensive shades, linebacker depth, fronts, or assignments may be based on the information from the script.  The script should include the following information:

- Down and distance
- Hash
- Formation
- Offensive play, left or right
- Yardage gained or lost

After the game, the script  can be very useful in the evaluation process.  The script can be helpful in evaluating player performance and assessing how well we dealt with the various offensive situations we encountered.  A coach can check the defensive calls made in terms of blitzes, coverages, and mistakes made by the staff or players.

The script should be saved for several reasons:

- It can be used for reference in a future game against the same opponent.
- You may face opponents with similar offenses.
- You may wish to trade this information with other schools when you need extra help preparing for an unfamiliar, out-of-the-area opponent in the playoffs.
- You should always keep files on your opponents.  You never know when you will face that team or coaching staff again.

During the game, the best time to talk to the players and make adjustments is in between series.  When adjustments are yelled at the players during play, it just confuses them and illustrates that they obviously weren't prepared properly.  I want our players and coaches to understand what we are trying to do. As a result, it may sometimes resemble a mini-coaching clinic on the sidelines during the game. I want our coaches communicating with the players, not just watching the game. Coaches need to coach, not spectate.  When no adjustments need to be made, the players may be given a pep talk or  a butt chewing as necessary.  A coach should keep in mind that a football game is no place for players to be in self-denial!

# Monterey High School Football Job Description for Assistant Coaches and Coordinators

### Assistant Football Coach

1. All coaches appointed by the principal will be governed by the following expectations:
   - All decisions will be made by the head coach unless otherwise stated.

2. Conduct
   - Good taste is recommended.
   - Keep in mind that you are representing Monterey High School at all times.

3. Designations
   - Every coach assigned is considered an assistant Varsity football coach.
   - The District's pay scale will be designated as:
     ❏ Frosh team coordinator
     ❏ Junior Varsity team coordinator

4. Responsibility on the Field
   - Teach necessary skills as designated (by position assignment).
   - Evaluate player personally
   - Communicate with:
     ❏ Head coach
     ❏ Coordinators
   - Provide necessary written communication.
   - Available to hold and share group meetings.
   - Plan and coordinate group's practice activities.
   - Assist coordinators:
     ❏ Form depth chart
     ❏ Assist in practice plan formation

❑ Assist in game plan preparation
❑ Review group's weekly performance on film
❑ Re-evaluation of groups
    —skills
    —effectiveness
    —mental attitudes
    —ability to perform under stress
❑ Carry out any assigned duties by coordinators
    —scout teams
    —written materials
- General record keeping as necessary by assigned groups.
❑ Records and reports to head coach or designated coach.

## 5. Staff Meetings
- Due to the nature of football, designated staff meetings will be held and all coaches involved are required to attend.
- Pre-opening of season:
❑ Designated days and times are determined by the head coach
- Post practice:
❑ During double sessions
    —post-practice meeting
    a. plan next day's practice
    b. general business
- Game week:
❑ Mondays, a.m.
    —5:30 a.m. at Monterey High School
    —entire staff
❑ Mondays, p.m.
    —Varsity staff
    a. 6:10 p.m.-varsity/team meeting
      √ Review films
      √ Review scouting report
    b. 7:00 p.m.-general staff meeting
      √ Game plans
      √ Week's practice plans
❑ Thursday, p.m.
    —varsity team meeting weekly at 7:00 p.m.
    a. site to be announced each week.
❑ Friday, noon/12:10 p.m.
    —varsity staff
❑ Post-game meetings
    —determined by the head coach by need

- Post season meetings:
  - ❏ Monthly meetings will be called
    - —dates/times are determined by the availability of the staff.
  - ❏ Purpose
    - —re-revaluation
    - —general planning

6. Adjunct Duties
   - Booster club:
     - ❏ Strongly suggested that each coach be a member
     - ❏ Meetings
       - —attendance optional
     - ❏ Social functions
       - —strongly suggest attendance
   - Fund raising:
     - ❏ Three main events are planned
       - —souvenir program ad sales
       - —fireworks stand
       - —Scottish games parking
     - ❏ Attendance and participation are strongly encouraged
     - ❏ Additional events may be planned according to need
   - Off-season weight room duty:
     - ❏ Coaches will be required to serve on a rotating basis by availability
       - —in case of absence, coach assigned will be responsible for finding a substitute.
     - ❏ Coaches are encouraged to participate to create a feeling of support to players
   - General duties:
     - ❏ Pre and post practice as assigned by head coach
       - —training room
       - —locker room
       - —field
       - —cage
     - ❏ Equipment issue and pickup
       - —All coaches are required to be in attendance.
     - ❏ Staff materials
       - —all equipment issued is the property of Monterey High School
       - a. re-issue
         - √ return of damaged items
       - b. Termination
         - √ return of all
         - * issued items
         - * written materials

❑ Keys

    —each coach will be responsible for his keys

    —off-campus personnel

    a. will return their keys at conclusion of season.

## Football Coordinators:

1. Will work under direct supervision of the head coach.

2. Will help develop the base game plan for designated area and/or plays to be put in:
   - Written communication to staff by the staff meeting.
   - Chair designated aspect of staff meeting for master game plan.
   - Determine the themes for the master practice plans as determined by the game plan.
   - Supply written final game plan by Thursday evening.

3. Will serve as the coach in charge of designated work team in his assigned area:
   - Necessary written communication
   - Staff assignments

4. Will fulfill the following amount of responsibility in a specific area:
   - Determined by the head coach:
   - ❑ Area of responsibility
     - —coordinator will have 49% control/authority.
       - √ head coach - 51%
     - —game determining situation
       - √ head coach decision
     - —position coaches
       - √ assist coordinator
   - ❑ Out of area
     - —participate as position coach
     - —provide assistance in relationship to his area of responsibility
   - ❑ Critical decisions
     - —made by head coach
       - √ equipment
       - √ personnel
       - √ staffing
       - √ game

5. Will be assigned to one of the following designated areas:
   - Varsity:
   - ❑ Offensive coordinator
   - ❑ Defensive coordinator
   - ❑ Special team coordinator

- Junior varsity game day:
  - ❏ Offensive play calling
    —under supervision of offensive coordinator
  - ❏ Defensive signal calling
    —under supervision of defensive coordinator
  - ❏ Special teams
    —to be split to pertain to assigned areas
- Freshmen:
  - ❏ Frosh team coordinator
    —coach in charge
  - ❏ Offensive coordinator
    —assigned by head coach
  - ❏ Defensive coordinator
    —assigned by head coach
  - ❏ Special team coordinator
    —assigned by head coach
- Scouting coordinator:
  - ❏ Assigned by head coach
  - ❏ Assign all scouting assignments to staff members according to availability

# Defensive Fronts:
# Alignments and Responsibilities

## Monterey High School

Defensive Front _____ 40 (Base)
Alignment/Responsibilities

| (Align) | Base | OPT | Drop B/C | Sprint Roll | Motion |
|---|---|---|---|---|---|
| **Def End** 9 Tech<br>Outside Shld Last Man Tight<br>On LOS. | Rd Stp<br>Squeeze Fld/Cont. | Attack<br>QB Too | Attack QB<br>Contain | Attack OB<br>Contain QB | N/A |
| **Def End** 9 Tech | Rd Stp<br>Squeeze Fwd Contain | Trail as Deep as Deepest<br>Back | Attack QB<br>Contain | Trail as Deep as Deepest<br>Back | N/A |
| **Def Tac** 3 Tech<br>Outside Eye Guard (to head<br>on Big Split) | Attack<br>B GAP through guard | Attack<br>Squeeze Dive By | Attack QB<br>Draw/Screen | Attack QB<br>Draw/Screen | N/A<br>unless unbalance |
| **Def Tac** 3 Tech<br>(Note Backside Play Hard<br>Trad/Ctr) | Depending<br>upon set I=FB | Play Hard Trap | Attack QB<br>Draw/Screen | Attack QB<br>Draw/Screen | N/A<br>unless unbalance |
| **Sam** 8 Tech<br>Head Up TE or TE to Strength | Rd Stp. Attack Up Fld<br>TB/Bk Away | Rd Stp<br>Attack Pitch | Flat | Flat | Bump |
| **Rover**-Split<br>Side-Head Up Slot or<br>Weakside TE or 2x2 Pro. | Rd Stp<br>Attack Up Fld<br>TB/Bk Away | Rd Stp<br>Pitch/Opt<br>Trap Bic Side | Flat | Flat | Bump<br>Widen accordingly |
| **Mike** Head Up<br>Guard-4yds Deep to Strg/TE<br>Side | Rd Stp \[Too\]<br>Attack B Gap<br>or off Tac/TB | Attack<br>Onside Dive Rd Stp | Rd Stp<br>Hook and Curl | Rd Stp<br>Hook and Curl | Bump<br>Visual |
| **Willy** Head Up<br>Guard 4 yds Deep | Rd Stp \[Away\]<br>Play Hard Backside Trap | Rd Stp Hard + Scrap Bic<br>Side | Rd Stp<br>Hook and Curl | Rd Stp<br>Hook and Curl | Bump<br>Visual |
| **Corner**<br>5 yds off Rec End of LOS<br>No closer than 5 yds to S.Line | Force \[Too\] | Pitch | Deep<br>Outside<br>1/3 | Deep<br>Outside<br>1/3 | Cover<br>on<br>Perimeter |
| **Safety**<br>Middle 8yds | Roll<br>Deep 1/2 | Roll<br>Deep 1/2 | Deep<br>Middle | Deep<br>Middle | N/A |
| **Corner**<br>5 yds off Rec End of LOS<br>No closer than 5 yds to S.Line | Roll \[Away\]<br>Deep 1/2 | Roll<br>Deep 1/2 | Deep<br>Outside 1/3 | Deep<br>Outside 1/3 | Cover on Perimeter |

**Monterey High School**

Defensive Front ___Base-40___
Coverage ___Green /Zone 3 Deep___
Alignment/Responsibility

| | Pro | Double TE Slot | Twin Wide | Trips | Double Wing | Motion |
|---|---|---|---|---|---|---|
| **Sam** Flat | Tight End Head Up | TE to Slot Head Up | TE Head Up | Bump to M Spot | Strong Side Wing Head Up | Bump Depending upon form |
| **Rover** Flat | Split Side 2x2 | Head Up Slot | Split D.F. Bet. Tac and Slot | #2 Rec (Inside) Head Up | Weak Side Slot | Bump (general to you) |
| **Mike** Curl and Hook | Head Up Guard 4 yds | Head Up Guard 4 yds | Head Up Guard 4 yds | Moves to W. Head Up 4 yds | Head Up Guard 4 yds | Bump |
| **Willy** Curl and Hook | Head Up Guard 4 yds | Head Up Guard 4 yds | Head Up Guard 4 yds | Head Up #3 (inside) Rec | Head Up Guard 4 yds | Bump |
| **Corner** Deep 1/3 | Inside Eye 5 yds off | Inside Eye 5yds off | SE No closer than 5 yds | SE Inside eye 5yds off | Inside Eye 5yds off | Widen off Perimeter |
| **Safety** Deep | Middle 8 yds | Middle 8 yds | Middle 8 yds | Shade to trips Guards outside eye | Middle | No effect |
| **Corner** Deep 1/3 | Inside Eye 5yds | SE 5 yds | TE 2yds outside 5 yds Deep | TE 2 yds off 5 yds Deep | Inside Eye SE 5 yds off | Widen on Perimeter |

## 40 Green vs.

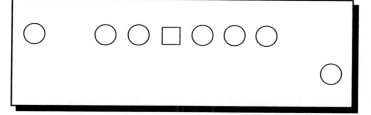

**PRO**

**DBL TE FIK**

**TWIN**

**TRIPS**

**DBL WG**

**Monterey High School**

Defensive Front___40_____
Coverage __Brown (Man under Free)__
Alignment/Responsibility

| | Pro | Double TE Slot | Twin Wide | Trips | Double Wing | Motion |
|---|---|---|---|---|---|---|
| **Sam** | Man TE | Man TE to FIK | Deal W/CB TE | Bump over to Mike Back | Wing to Strength Man | Bump to next man except pro |
| **Rover** | Free Banjo Backout | Free Banjo Backout | #2 Rec Man | Inside #2 Rec Man | Wing away from strength man | Bump widen to corner |
| **Mike** | RB Man | RB Man | RB Man | Inside #3 Rec Man | Man RB Deal w/w | Bump accordingly (cover trips) |
| **Willy** | RB Banjo BK to Rover | RB Banjo BK to Rover | RB Man | Remain RB Man | Man RB Deal with Man | Bump accordingly |
| **Corner** | #1 Rec to Side Man | #1 Rec to Side Man | #1 Rec to Side Man | #1 Rec to Side Man | #1 Rec to Side Man | Bump Cover on outside |
| **Safety** | Free | Free | Free | Free | Free | Free |
| **Corner** | #1 Rec to Side Man | #1 Rec to Side Man deal CB w/ Sam | #1 Rec to Side Man CB deal w/ Sam | #1 Rec to Side Man | #1 Rec to Side Man | Bump Cover on Outside (A formation change) |

## 40 Brown vs.

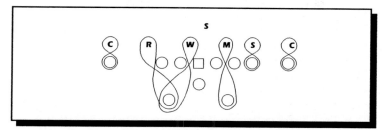

**PRO**

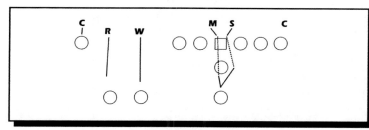

**DBL TE FIK**

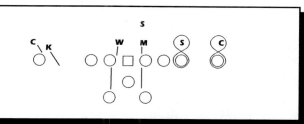

**TWIN WIDE**

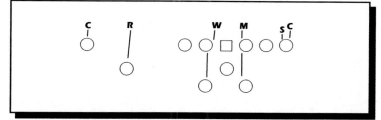

**TRIPS**

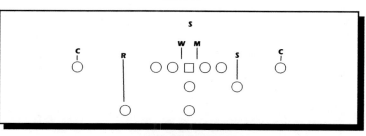

**DBL WG**

## Monterey High School

Defensive Front__40_____
Coverage  __White/5 under Man 2 deep__
Alignment/Responsibility

| | Pro | Double TE Slot | Twin Wide | Trips | Double Wing | Motion |
|---|---|---|---|---|---|---|
| **Sam** | Curl Rush | TE to FIK Flat | Flat | Hang Curl/Flat | | |
| **Rover** | Flat | Flat | Curl | Flat | | |
| **Mike** | Hook and Curl | Hook and Curl | Hook and Curl | Curl | Wipe Coverage to Brown or Green | |
| **Willy** | Hook and Curl | Hook and Curl | Hook and Curl | Hook | | |
| **Corner** | To TE FIK Flat | To FIK Flat | Flat | To Trips Deep 1/2 | | |
| **Safety** | Deep 1/2 to FIkside | Deep 1/2 to FIkside | Deep 1/2 to SE/side | Deep 1/2 | | |
| **Corner** | Deep 1/2 to SE | Deep 1/2 away FIK | To TE Deep 1/2 | Away Flat | | |

*Note: motion changes the formation.*
*Rotate according to motion or wipe and go to Brown.*

# 40 White vs.

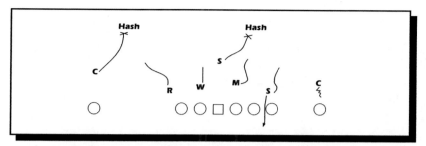

**PRO**

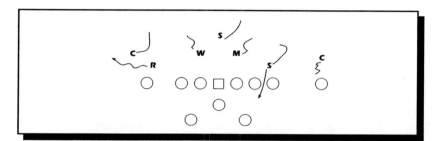

**DBL TE FIK**

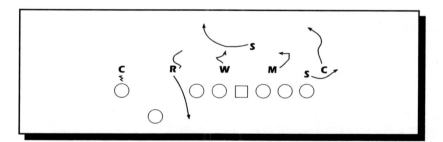

**TWIN**

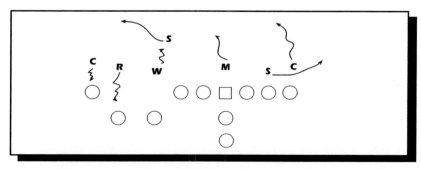

**TRIPS**

## Monterey High School

Defensive Front <u>  40            </u>
Coverage <u>  Gold/5 under Man 2 deep  </u>
Alignment/Responsibility

| | Pro | Double TE Slot | Twin Wide | Trips | Double Wing | Motion |
|---|---|---|---|---|---|---|
| **Sam** | TE Man | TE Man | TE Man | TE Man | Slot to Strength Man | Bump |
| **Rover** | Deep 1/2 Free Away from FIK | TE Man | Slot Man | 2nd Rec Man | Deep 1/2 Free (Float) | Bump |
| **Mike** | RB Man | RB Man | RB Man | RB 3rd Rec Man | Slot away from Sam Man | |
| **Willy** | RB Man | RB Man | RB Man | RB Man | RB Man | |
| **Corner** | SE/FIK Man | To FIK FIKMan | SE Man | SE to Trips Man | SE Man | |
| **Safety** | Deep 1/2 Free to FIk | Deep 1/2 to Strength Free | Deep 1/2 Two Rec | Deep 1/2 to Trips | Deep 1/2 to Strength | |
| **Corner** | SE/FIK Man | Away FIK Deep 1/2 Free | To TE Deep 1/2 Free | Deep 1/2 Free Away from Trips | SE Man | ↓ X |

X—Motion is only a formation change.

# 40 Gold vs.

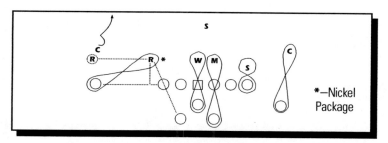

**PRO**

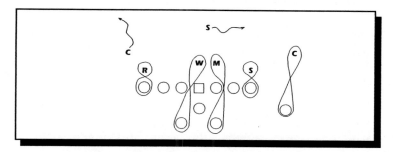

**DBL TE FIK**

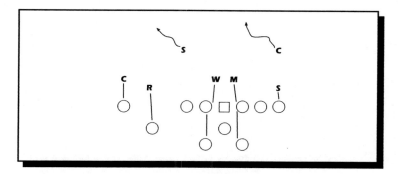

**TWIN WIDE**

## 40 Gold vs.

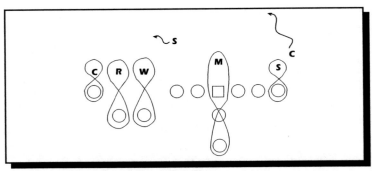

**TRIPS**

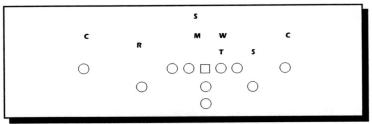

**WIDE GO TO BROWN**

## Monterey High School

Defensive Front __44__
Coverage _Same coverage as 40-Prevent_
Alignment/Responsibility

| | Base | OPT | Drop B/C | Sprint Roll | Motion |
|---|---|---|---|---|---|
| **Def End**<br>Normal 40 Base | | | All Responsibility Same | | |
| **Def End**<br>Normal 40 Base | | | As 40-Alignment | | |
| **Def Tac**<br>Normal 40 Base | | | Change—generally | | |
| **Def Tac**<br>Normal 40 Base | | | To get to pass drops | | |
| **Sam** Stack<br>Def End<br>To strength | | | | | |
| **Rover Stack**<br>Def End | | | | | |
| **Mike** Stack<br>Tac-4yds | | | | | |
| **Willy** Stack<br>Tac 4yds | | | | | |
| **Corner** 40<br>Normal<br>Base | | | | | |
| **Safety** 40<br>Normal<br>Base | | | | | |
| **Corner** 40<br>Normal<br>Base | | | | | |

Loose —The linebackers start with a 7-yard drop;
the corners start 10 yards deep, while the
safety is 15 yards deep.

**Monterey High School**

Defensive Front___50___
Coverage _____
Alignment/Responsibility

| | Base | OPT | (Green) Drop B/C | Sprint Roll | Motion |
|---|---|---|---|---|---|
| **Def End** Normal 40 | Normal | Attack QB | Contain Attack QB | Contain Attack QB | N/A |
| **Def End** Normal 40 | Normal | Attack QB | Contain Attack QB | | N/A |
| **Def Tac** To Strength TE/Tac-C Gap | C Gap Control | Dive BK too trap away | Attack QB | Attack QB | N/A |
| **Def Tac** Away Stength Normal | B Gap Control Hard Back Side Trap | Dive too Trap away | Screen Draw | Screen Draw | N/A |
| **Sam** Normal to 4yd Stack | Attack Flow Key | Pitch | Flat | Flat | Bump |
| **Rover** 4yds at O.T. | Attack Flow Key | Pitch | Flat | Flat | Bump |
| **Mike** 4 yds-Head Up center or stack | Attack Flow Key | Dive Block | Deep Middle of Hook and Bump | Deep Middle Shake to Curl Zone | Bump |
| **Willy** 3pt Stance, A Gap to strength | Up Field Attack QB | Up Field Back Up Mesh | Sack QB | Sack QB | N/A |
| **Corner** 5yd Normal | Normal | Too pitch | Deep Out 1/3 | Deep Out 1/3 | Bump |
| **Safety** 8 yd Normal | Normal | Roll to Pursuit | Deep Mid 1/3 | Deep Mid 1/3 | Bump |
| **Corner** 5 yd Normal | Normal | Away Roll to Pursuit | Deep Out 1/3 | Deep Out 1/3 | Bump |

**Monterey High School**

Defensive Front ___50___
Coverage ___Green (Zone)___
Alignment/Responsibility

| | Pro | Double TE Slot | Twin Wide | Trips | Double Wing | Motion |
|---|---|---|---|---|---|---|
| **Sam** | Flat | Flat | Flat Hang Don't cover grass | Hang Curl Zone | Flat Wg to Strength | |
| **Rover** | Flat | Flat | Flat Twin Side | #2 Rec Flat | Flat to Strength Wg | |
| **Mike** | Deep Mid Hook and Curl | Deep Mid to strength Hook and Curl | Hook and Curl to Twin | #3 Rec Hook and Curl | Deep Mid Hook and Curl | |
| **Willy** | Sack QB | Sack QB | Sack QB | Sack QB | Sack QB | N/A |
| **Corner** | Deep 1/3 Out | Deep 1/3 Out | Deep 1/3 Out | Deep 1/3 Out | Deep 1/3 Out | |
| **Safety** | Deep 1/3 Mid | Deep 1/3 Mid | Deep 1/3 Mid | Deep 1/3 Mid | Deep 1/3 Mid | |
| **Corner** | Deep 1/3 Out | Deep 1/3 Out | Deep 1/3 Out | Deep 1/3 Out | Deep 1/3 Out | |

## 50 Green vs.

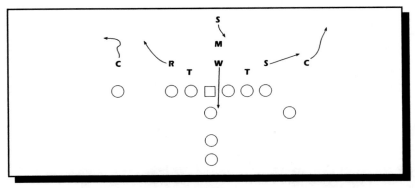

**PRO**

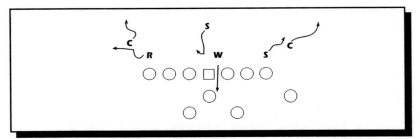

**DBL TE FIK**

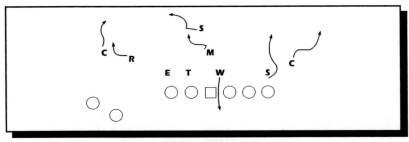

**TWIN WIDE**

## 50 Green vs.

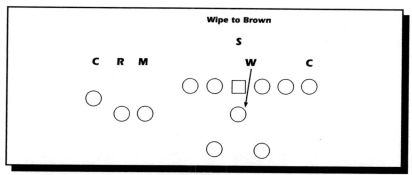

**TRIPS**

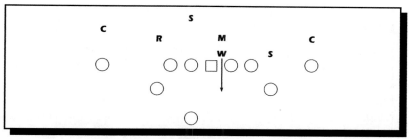

**DBL WG**

## Monterey High School

Defensive Front ____50____
Coverage ____Brown (Man under Free)____
Alignment/Responsibility

| | Pro | Double TE Slot | Twin Wide | Trips | Double Wing | Motion | |
|---|---|---|---|---|---|---|---|
| **Sam** | TE Man | TE Man to FIK Slot-RB/Rush | Rush | RB Man | Wg to Strength | | |
| **Rover** | RB Man | RB Away From FIK | Slot Man | Rec #2 Rec Man | Wg St. | | |
| **Mike** | RB Man | RB Man | RB Man | Rec #3 Man | RB Man | Bump-Adjust-to Formation | |
| **Willy** | Sack QB | Sack QB | Sack QB | Sack QB | Sack QB | | N/A |
| **Corner** | FIK/SE Man | FIK Man | SE Man | SE Man | SE Man | | |
| **Safety** | Free | Free | Free | Free | Free | | |
| **Corner** | FIK/SE Man | TE Man | TE Man | TE Man | SE Man | | |

## 50 Brown vs.

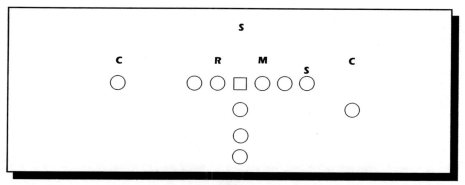

**PRO**

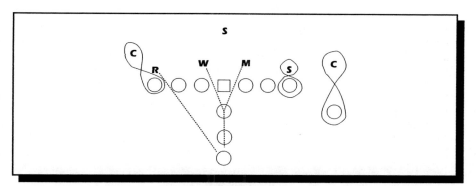

**DBL TE**

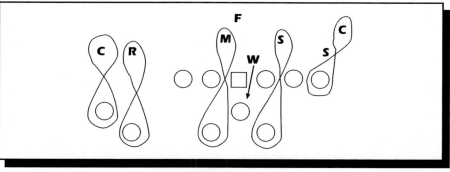

**TWIN**

# 50 Brown vs.

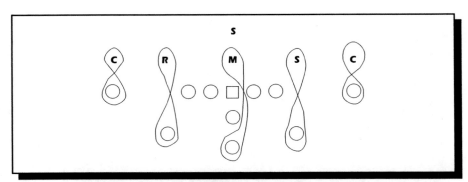

**TRIPS**

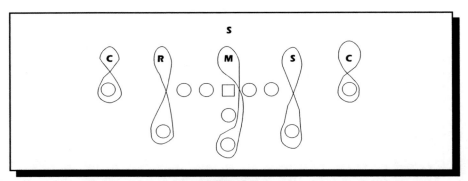

**DBL WG**

## Monterey High School

Defensive Front____60_____
Coverage ____Green_____
Alignment/Responsibility

|  | Pro | Double TE Slot | Twin Wide | Trips | Double Wing | Motion |
|---|---|---|---|---|---|---|
| **Sam** | Flat | Flat | Flat | Flat | Flat | |
| **Rover** | Flat | Flat | Flat | Flat | Flat | |
| **Mike** | Hook and Curl | Hook and Curl | Hook and Curl | Hook and Curl | Hook and Curl | Bump-Align-Change in accord w/ formation change |
| **Willy** | Hook and Curl | Hook and Curl | Hook and Curl | Hook and Curl | Hook and Curl | |
| **Corner** | Deep Out 1/3 | Deep Out 1/3 | Deep Out 1/3 | Deep Out 1/3 | Deep Out 1/3 | |
| **Safety** | Deep Mid 1/3 | Deep Mid 1/3 | Deep Mid 1/3 | Deep Mid 1/3 | Deep Mid 1/3 | |
| **Corner** | Deep 1/3 | Deep Out 1/3 | Deep Out 1/3 | Deep Out 1/3 | Deep Out 1/3 | Out |

## 60 Green vs.

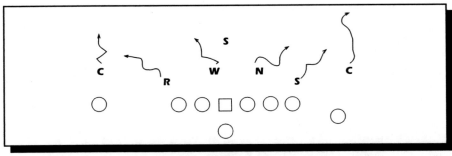

**PRO**

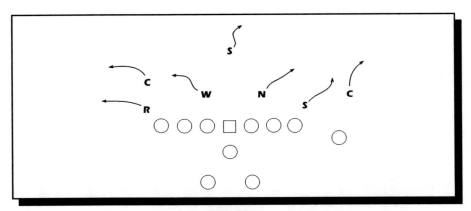

**DBL FIK**

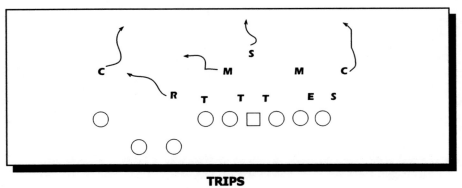

**TRIPS**

*—Wipe 40 Brown

**60 Green vs.**

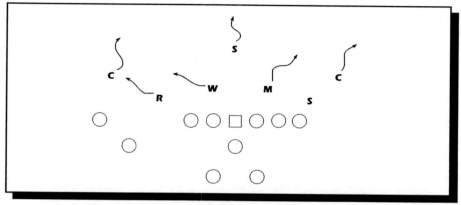

**TWIN**

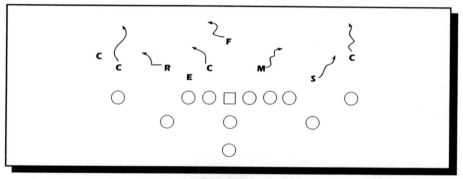

**DBL WG**

## Monterey High School

Defensive Front___60___
Coverage _____
Alignment/Responsibility

|  | Base | OPT | Drop B/C | Sprint Roll | Motion |
|---|---|---|---|---|---|
| **Def End**<br>C Gap<br>3pt Stance | Up Fld<br>Maintain Out-<br>side Leverage | Up<br>Fld to QB | Contain<br>QB<br>Rush QB | Contain<br>QB<br>Rush QB | N/A |
| **Def End**<br>C Gap<br>3pt Stance | Up Fld<br>Maintain Out-<br>side leverage | Up<br>Fld to QB | Contain<br>QB<br>Rush QB | Contain<br>QB<br>Rush QB | N/A |
| **Def Tac**<br>A Gap | Up Fld<br>Heel Depth | Dive BK/Hard<br>Trap Backside | QB<br>Screen/Draw | QB<br>Screen/Draw | N/A |
| **Def Tac**<br>A Gap | Up Fld<br>Heel Depth | Dive BK/Hard<br>Trap Backside | QB<br>Screen/Draw | QB<br>Screen/Draw | N/A |
| **Sam**<br>Outside shoulder<br>Last Man LOS | Squeeze<br>Attack<br>Cont. | Pitch<br>Hard Trap<br>Backside | Flat | Flat | Bump |
| **Rover**<br>Outside shoulder<br>Last Man LOS | Squeeze<br>Attack<br>Cont. | Pitch<br>Hard Trap<br>Backside | Flat | Flat | Bump |
| **Mike**<br>Head Up G 4yds | Near Back<br>Flow | Dive<br>Hard Trap<br>Backside | Hook and Curl | Hook and Curl | Bump |
| **Willy**<br>Head Up G 4yds | Near Back<br>Flow | Dive /Hard Trap<br>Backside | Hook and Curl | Hook and Curl | Bump |
| **Corner**<br>Normal 5 yds | Deep 1/3<br>out Force | Pitch | Deep<br>Out 1/3 | Deep<br>Out 1/3 | Widen on<br>Perimeter |
| **Safety**<br>8 yds | Deep 1/3<br>Mid-roll | Roll<br>to<br>Pursuit | Deep<br>Mid 1/3 | Deep<br>Mid |  |
| **Corner**<br>Normal 8 yds | Deep 1/3<br>out Force | Roll to<br>Pursuit/Play | Deep<br>Out 1/3 | Deep<br>Out 1/3 | Widen on<br>Perimeter |

## Monterey High School

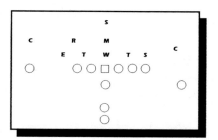

Defensive Front  30-Defense
Coverage _____
Alignment/Responsibility

|  | Base | OPT | Drop B/C | Sprint Roll | Motion |
|---|---|---|---|---|---|
| **Def End** Normal | Normal 40 | QB Trail | Rush | Rush | N/A |
| **Def End** Normal | Normal 40 | QB Trail | Rush | Rush | N/A |
| **Def Tac** Outside Eye G | Normal 40 | Dive BK Trap | Rush | Rush | N/A |
| **Def Tac** Outside Eye G | Normal 40 | Dive BK Trap | Rush | Rush | N/A |
| **Sam** Normal Head Up TE | Attack Key | Pitch | Flat | Flat | Bump According to rules |
| **Rover** Normal 2x2 or Head Up TE/Slot | Attack Key | Pitch | Flat | Flat | Bump |
| **Mike** Stacked Behind Willy | Attack Key | Dive BK | Middle | Middle | Do Not Move |
| **Willy** Head Center 3 pt Stance | Blitz A Gap Strength | Blitz A Gap Strength | Blitz A Gap Strength | Blitz A Gap Strength | N/A |
| **Corner** *Normal | | | Out 1/3 | Out 1/3 | Bump |
| **Safety** Normal | | | Mid 1/3 | Mid 1/3 | Bump |
| **Corner** Normal | | | Out 1/3 | Out 1/3 | Bump |

* Switch — Willy drop, Mike fine.

## Monterey High School

Defensive Front____60____
Coverage_____Brown_____
Alignment/Responsibility

| | Pro | Double TE Slot | Twin Wide | Trips | Double Wing | Motion |
|---|---|---|---|---|---|---|
| **Sam** | TE Man | TE to FIK Man | Rush Banjo Back | Banjo Back to Side Rush | Wg to Strength Man | Bump |
| **Rover** | Rush Banjo Back Side | Rush Banjo Back to | Slot Man | #2 Rec Man | Wg away man | Change to Formation |
| **Mike** | RB Man | RB Man | RB Man | #3 Rec Man | RB Man Rush | |
| **Willy** | RB Man | RB Man | RB Man | RB Man | RB Man Rush | |
| **Corner** | SE/FIK Man | TE away FIK Man | SE Man | SE Man | SE Man | |
| **Safety** | Free | Free | Free | Free | Free | |
| **Corner** | SE/FIK Man | TE away FIK Man | TE away away SE Man | TE away Man | SE Man | |

Note: This front is a very poor choice in a short-distance situation.

## 60 Brown vs.

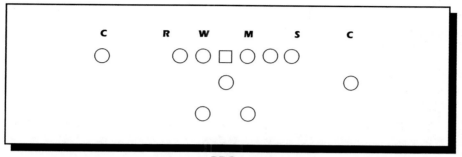

**PRO**

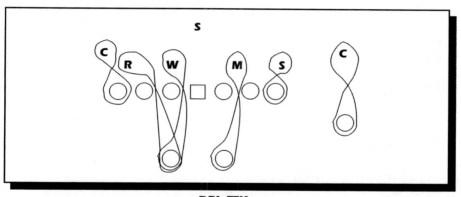

**DBL FIK**

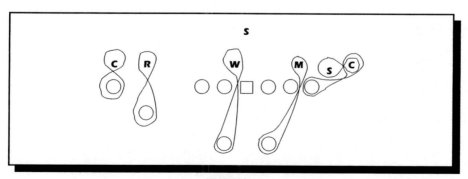

**TWIN***

* Banjo Back from M to Sam.

## 60 Brown vs.

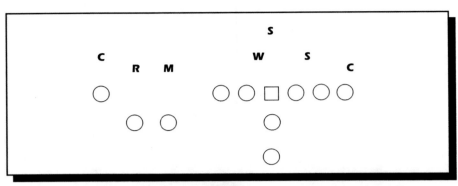

**TRIPS**

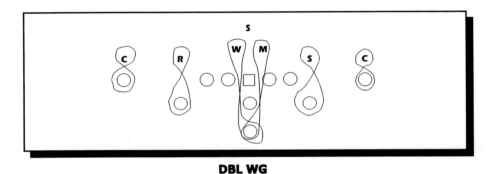

**DBL WG**

Coverage:

- Nickel package:
  Rover — replaced by 4th D.B. or next best pass defender.
  Note: He still has run support. A key coaching point is that you must run at Nickel so he's comfortable in practice.

- Dime package:
  Rover — replaced by 4th D.B. or next best pass defender.
  Dime — replaced by 5th D.B. or next best pass defender.
  Note — Both Nickel and Dime have run responsible (same as O.L.B. they replace).

# Linebacker Running Back Keys

| Formation/ Linebacker | I | Split | Strong | Weak | Bone | Pwr I |
|---|---|---|---|---|---|---|
| **Sam** | TB | Far Back Cross | FB | HB | Cross to Far BK | TB to Pwr IBK |
| **Rover** | TB | Far Back | HB | FB | Cross to Far BK | TB to Pwr IBK |
| **Mike** | FB | Near Back | HB | FB | FB to Near BK | FB |
| **Willy** | FB | Near Back | FB | HB | FB to Near BK | Pwr IBK to FB |

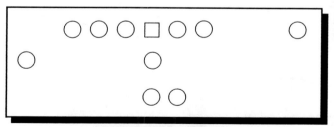

**Weakside Formation**

# Sample Defensive Script Sheet Form

| Yd Line | Down Dist. | Formation | Play | Gain Loss | +/- Comment | +/- Comment | +/- Comment |
|---------|------------|-----------|------|-----------|-------------|-------------|-------------|
|         |            |           |      |           |             |             |             |
|         |            |           |      |           |             |             |             |
|         |            |           |      |           |             |             |             |
|         |            |           |      |           |             |             |             |
|         |            |           |      |           |             |             |             |
|         |            |           |      |           |             |             |             |

# APPENDIX E

## Sample Completed Defensive Script Sheet Form

| Yd Line | Down Dist. | Formation | Play | Gain Loss | +/- Comment | +/- Comment | +/- |
|---|---|---|---|---|---|---|---|
| 32 | 1ST | 40 GRN | DIVE RT | | 1+ | 1+ | |
| 33 | 2ND | 40 GRN TG | | | PASS COMP | 10+ | |
| 41/43 | 1ST | 40 GRN TG | POWER LEFT | | 1 | 14+ | |
| 43 | 1ST | 40 GR TG | DIVE RT | | 7+ | 7+ | |
| 40/35 | 2ND | 40 GRN TG | TRAP LEFT | | 5+ | 5+ | |
| 40 | 3RD | 40 GRN TG | | | INCOMPLETE | | |

| Yd Line | Down Dist. | Formation | Play | Gain Loss | +/- Comment | +/- Comment | +/- Comment |
|---|---|---|---|---|---|---|---|
| 23 | 1ST | 40 GRN | | | POWER LEFT | Ø | |
| 24 | 2ND | 40 GRN | | | PASS COMP | 13+ | |
| 10 | 1ST | 40 GRN | #5 | POWER RT | 2+ | 2+ | |
| 8 | 2ND | 40 GRN | #5 | 5+ | POWER LEFT | 5+ | |
| 3 | 3RD | GL | #44 | | DIVE LEFT | 3+ | |
| 5 | 1ST | 40 GRN WF | POWER LEFT | | | Ø+ | |

| Yd Line | Down Dist. | Formation | Play | Gain Loss | +/- Comment | +/- Comment | +/- Comment |
|---|---|---|---|---|---|---|---|
| 5 | 2ND 40 GRN MF | | | PASS INCOMP | | | |
| 5 | 3RD 40 GRN MF | | | PASS INCOMP. | | | |
| 35 | 1ST 40 GRN MF | | FAKE | DIVE PASS | BROKEN 0 | | |
| 35 | 2ND 40 GRN WF | | | PASS INCOMP | 0 | | |
| 35 | 3RD 40 GRN | | | SCREEN LEFT | 15+ | | |
| 50 | 1ST 40 GRN MF | | | POWER LEFT | −5 | | |

Pete Noble is a teacher and former head football coach at Monterey High School in Monterey, California. Prior to holding his position at M.H.S., Coach Noble served as the head football coach at Encinal High School in Alameda, California. He has 16 years experience as a head football coach, with a career won/loss record of 119-53-3. He has been recognized seven times with Coach-of-the-Year honors. A noted speaker and clinician, Coach Noble has traveled the country studying college and professional level programs, as well as sharing ideas about the split 4-4 defense and the split-back veer option offense, both of which he has very successfully refined at Monterey. An avid and accomplished surfer, Coach Noble maintains an extensive collection of vintage surfboards at his home in Monterey, where he resides with his wife, Cathy and their two children—daughter Jaime and son Garin.

James A. Peterson, Ph.D., is a free-lance writer who resides in Monterey, California with his wife, Susan. A 1966 graduate of the University of California at Berkeley, Peterson served on the faculty of the United States Military Academy at West Point for 16 years. A prolific writer, Peterson has written or co-authored 81 books and more than 150 published articles. A Fellow of the American College of Sports Medicine, he has appeared on several national television shows, including ABC's Good Morning America, The CBS Evening News, ABC's Nightline, and The Home Show.